The Role of a Parent in the Sex Education of their Child

Breaking the silence and ignorance
Removing the taboos
Preventing the abuses

Astrid Mutha SONI

The biblical quotations from this book are, for the most part, taken from the revised version of 1910 Louis Segond, unless otherwise specified and directly next to the references.

The Role of the Parent in the Sex Education of their Child

First edition © 2020 by Astrid M. Soni

Publisher

Grave la Vision

www.RESTORATIONTOP.NET

www.sonirestorationministries.org

Table of Contents

Virgin, Naïve and Vulnerable **9**

PART ONE: **Concept, Framework and Limits**

Chap. I. Sexuality, a gift from God**17**
Chap. II. Why give sex educationto your child?**22**
Chap. III. The concept of sex education and sexual abuse **28**
Chap. IV. At what age should a child start sex education?**34**
Chap. V. The family, a suitable place for sex education **41**
Chap. VI. The silence of parents **52**
Chap. VII. The harm of silence**67**
Chap. VIII. Sex education for girls instead of circumcision**73**
Chap. IX. Beyond food and clothing**78**
Chap. X. The error of giving sex education by talking only about sex**85**
Chap. XI. What sex education is not ?**88**

PART TWO: **Practical Topics to Address**

Chap. XII. Different subjects to be discussed in the sexual education of the child**104**
Chap. XIII. Preliminaries**110**
Chap. XIV. Nudity and pornography**119**
Chap. XV. External influence**124**

Chap. XVI. Self-esteem*128*
Chap. XVII. Body changes related to puberty*133*
Chap. XVIII. Virginity*142*
Chap. XIX. Sexual relationships*146*
Chap. XX. Love without sex*151*
Chap. XXI. Friendships*154*
Chap. XXII. Twelve golden rules that every parent should know*156*

One more word*159*
The path to healing*160*

DEDICATION

I dedicate this book:

- To all parents who love their children and want to educate them, to protect them from all forms of sexual abuse

- To all the women who took part in our conferences and who presented the desire to know what to really say when we want to give good sex education.

- To all mothers in the world; those who have a desire to impart a full education to their children, but who are limited by ignorance and taboos. Let this book serve as inspiration and a workbook.

- To families and cultures who think that certain practices such as circumcision or castration are a way of protecting their children. Find in this book why we think that sex education for children is the best alternative.

- To young boys and girls who are preparing for marriage so that they become equipped parents, who are able to assume their task well.

- To leaders of different youth groups and ministries, who have the responsibility of educating the masses.

- To any person, man or woman who has been the victim of any form of sexual abuse, in order to find a cure to, in turn, become an educator.

- To our children: Debbie, Salem, Creisson, and Rosette whom we love with all our hearts, tobecome equipped parents, proud to teach and educate their children without taboos.

ACKNOWLEDGMENTS

I thank my parents who by the grace of God made me what I am today and made me grow in the way of the Lord in a very harmonious home.

With all my heart, I would like to thank Emmanuel Soni Mukwenze, my dear husband and friend, for our thirty years of marriage, which have been a complete education where we learned from each other, not only to know each other to live in harmony, but also to educate our children by having frank and taboo-free conversations. His contribution is incalculable. Despite his multiple occupations, he deprived himself of hours of sleep to help with proofreading, the layout and presentation of the cover of this book.

I thank the beloved Steve L. Panza, for his very commendable contribution in the proofreading of this work. He was my high school English teacher; his course was my favorite course, for which I always had very excellent grades. The Lord has given us the grace to lead Steve in the way of the Lord, and since then, the relationship 'of a teacher and his pupil' has given way to brotherhood in Christ. He is a man of God who influences many lives and who is a blessing for the Body of Christ.

Thank you to Neliana Lord for her encouragement.

My thanks go to the women and men, who took part in our conferences and who, by their eagerness and desires, inspired me to put these lessons in writing in order to serve a greater audience.

Parenting and Sex Education
Breaking the silence and ignorance
Challenging and removing the taboos
Preventing and healing the abuses

This book is
a bold stand with a tender tone
forancient values and modern common senses
in a context where empiric taboos
and liberal caprices collide mercilessly.

"You pity the plant,
for which you did not labor,
nor did you make it grow, which came
into being in a night and perished in a night.
And should not I pity Nineveh, that great city,
in which there are more than 120,000
persons who do not know their right hand
from their left, and also much cattle?"
(Jonah 4:10,11English Standard Version)

The Publisher
Grave la Vision

Naive, virgin and vulnerable

 I grew up in a close-knit Christian family, where relationships with my parents were very close, with great love and without conflict. My father had studied theology at Valley Forge in the state of Pennsylvania in the United States. So, we grew up in a family open to other cultures; however talking about sexuality had never been the subject of a single conversation with us as a family. I had never been warned of physiological changes from puberty until adulthood. My world seemed well protected that I was not aware that there were malicious people in this world who wanted to sexually abuse others.

At the age of 12, my parents sent me to live with my sister for two years, 74 miles from where they lived. All I took

Protection is not complete if it is only a series of prohibitions without instructions

from their instructions was that in order to be a good girl, I should not befriend a boy. Something that I scrupulously observed.

In September 1978, my elder brother Matthew and I were ready to go to boarding school to start the school year. My brother had been studying there for several years, and I was going there for the first time. Our school was located a few hundred kilometers from the city where the family lived. The road trips took several days since our parents decided to make us travel by river.

We got into this boat, which was called an "outboard", which in fact was a large motorized canoe with a roof. The boat could take up to several dozen people. So we left for more than twenty-four hours of travel, going up the Kwilu river. It was a long journey with several adults, unknown people. But no doubt, my parents knew that this little boat would get us to our destination "safely".

I had just turned 16 and, in the past, I had already had the experience of traveling with my parents, in a large, very luxurious boat, where we were staying in first class, with very bright rooms and well-made beds. At each meal time, the bell invited first class travelers to go to the ship's restaurant to eat. The chefs were dressed in white and served food to all passengers. It was a great experience that I wanted to relive.

Unfortunately in this motorized canoe, things were very different. People were crammed next to each other. There was not enough space, hence our mobility was very limited. This large pirogue which carried several bags of foodstuffs, did not sail at very high speed. The beautiful view of the forest along the river captured my attention, as well as the other boats that passed us or that went the opposite direction. Sometimes we saw a fisherman alone on a smaller canoe in the middle of the river. The trip was made by a lot of pretty things I experienced for the first time.

As night approached everything went dark, it was impossible to continue sailing, because the visibility was almost zero. The boat had docked by the river for the night. There was dead silence. You could hear the soft sound of the flowing water, and the different insects that whistled in their own way in the grass by the river. The experience was both interesting and terrifying. I have never been so close to water in my life. And what can I say about spending the night on a canoe in the water? But as our parents reassured us that the trip would be safe, it kept us at peace.

Each traveler found a small space to lie down. I also put myself in the middle of people lying down, not knowing that it would be the longest night of my life; a night when I will be unable to close my eyes.

As my parents trusted this boat, I didn't fear anything and I started to doze off to sleep. Suddenly, I felt a hand that occasionally tapped on my thighs, advancing towards my buttocks, as if someone was looking for something. When

I moved, that hand moved away and after a moment when I tried to sleep again, the same scene was repeated.

I began to understand that someone intentionally wanted to abuse me and I started to move all night to deter him. I was impatiently waiting for dawn, because I told myself that no one would have the courage to behave like this in the daytime.

A horrible experience, but I kept silent until the morning without shouting for help or denouncing this malicious hand which wanted to harm me. I was afraid to draw such attention to myself; what would have happened to me if the other travelers refused to believe me?

In the early morning I could not share my trauma with anyone; and not even with my brother who was my closest traveling companion. The reason for my silence was simple: topics like this had never been the subject of family conversations.

Today with hindsight I understand that I was a good girl for my parents, I was a virgin but ignorant about it, that is to say uneducated, and therefore vulnerable...

Like me, many children today are thrown into society without parents taking the time to educate them about the reality of their sexuality and they become easy prey for sexual abuse.

We recommend that every parent read this book or take the online sex education course we teach.

The subject of sexuality is almost taboo in the family and in most cultures. It is a subject which several parents have been unable or unwilling to discuss freely with their children. Some lack skills which can help to offer such an exchange, while for others, this subject embarrasses, and to speak about it in family seems to be a lack of modesty.

Our effort is to seek not only to show the dangers that are linked to ignorance and silence about sexual abuse, but above all to pinpoint possible solutions and strategies that any parent can put in place to ensure the sex education of their child.

The incident I have just told you about was not the first I faced in my childhood.

The girl who had her first period at school

I remember a scene that happened when I was still in elementary school. A girl had her period, probably it was her first period, either because it was early or because she was a little older than the other students. Unfortunately, her skirt was stained with blood. So at the end of the classes, when she was walking, a crowd of students, boys and girls, followed her very closely, curious to see what had happened to her, knowing that she had not hurt herself. Some came running to see what was going on and the group was only growing. To this day I wonder why there was no adult to disperse these students and free the little girl? At times she was using her notebook to cover behind her skirt, but as you can imagine it slowed her down and she could not keep her hand back for a long time. It should be noted that here there were no school buses, or parents who came to pick up their children by car. She therefore had to walk a long distance to return home to her family. At the same time, I would like to open a little parenthesis to say that in that year in the school I attended, I do not remember having female teachers. Who knows, maybe a female teacher would have treated the situation differently. And presumably, her parents had never told her about these changes in puberty, so the fear and the confusion in this girl's head must have been absolute. If all of us had received some family sex education, I think the scene would be different, and especially the teachers would have saved the little girl from experiencing such embarrassment.

Today I believe that through my services, I am paying my debt for not being able to help this friend, simply because I too was ignorant, never having been prepared. If my writing and my lessons can simply prevent such scenes, I would be happy.

PART ONE

CONCEPT, FRAMEWORK AND LIMITS

In this Part, we will tackle the concepts of sexuality, sex education and sexual abuse.

Deciding on the importance of the family environment as an appropriate framework to approach this marvelous subject, we will discuss why many parents do not dare to play their role of sex educators of the children whom God has placed under their parental care.

Despite certain repetitions purposely made in these lines, we will also have to specify that by this work we are committed to circumscribing our approach without pretending to exhibit all our expertise on such vital subjects as sexuality, education, family and even parenting. We are aware that we are not necessarily speaking to specialists but to ordinary people to whom God has entrusted this multidimensional task of parenting in a constantly changing world, full of taboos.

Chapter I.

Let us face it, sexuality is a subject that is very little discussed in most families. For some, out of fear as it has always been a taboo subject, and for others out of modesty, because they consider sexuality to be a source of depravity, hence an evil. As I read the Holy Scriptures, I came to understand that God does not hold back from addressing this subject in His Word. Whole chapters give a guideline on how His people should experience their sexuality.

Sexuality is not an invention of the devil

Sexuality is not an invention of the devil; it is

Sexualityemanatesf romGod

rather a gift from God. Every believer has to understand that sexuality is holy and pure; every child of God has to experience their sexuality for the glory of God. It is when sexuality is perverted that it becomes a sin and contrary to the will of God.

In the beginning when God created man and woman, the Bible says: *"God blessed them, and God said unto them, be fruitful, multiply, fill the earth"* (Genesis 1:27-28) See Genesis 2:18; 4:1

Adam and Eve had no other way to fill the earth if not by experiencing their sexuality. God sealed the union of man and woman by giving them the freedom to experience their sexuality and to perpetuate the human race.

In Genesis 4:1 when Adam sexually knew his wife Eve, the Bible says that Eve conceived and bore their first son, Cain. At the sight of this blessing, Eve exclaims to say, *"I have formed a man with the help of the Lord"* (Genesis 4:1). Eve does not attribute their sexuality to Satan, but to God, with whose help they had a child. Sexuality is not evil, it is divine and, God must be the only one to teach us how to experience it.

Many parents don't want to hear about sex education because they do

> **Parents or schoolduty ?**

not have a divine perspective on the subject. They believe it is the school's duty to give this education to their children; and they do not even bother to learn the content of this course on sex education that the school offers. And yet sex education is also called "life education" or "family education", which means that it should also be given as a family. How would a parent who has the duty to educate their child give this to a third person to introduce their child to the basic realities of life?

In this book we bring an approach according to the Word of God. Each parent will discover their share of responsibility and the equipment necessary for them to proudly introduce their child to the essentials of life.

Statistics on sexual abuse of children are reaching epidemic and worrying proportions today. This is because parents don't fulfill their duty to educate their children on time. Children are abused by family, at school or with friends, by strangers or relatives, without the knowledge of the parents who are supposed to protect them. Parents' refusal to speak to their children about sex education will not prevent them from receiving it in a diffuse manner; the street unfortunately will offer it to them effortlessly. But at what cost?

From ancient times, parents believed that it was the school's responsibility to give this education to their children. Yet very few know the content of what the school teaches their children. The approach or purpose that the Christian parent pursues in giving this education is not necessarily that which the school pursues. We will talk about it in detail in the following lines.

Many children who are sexually abused do not report their abusers because there is a culture of silence that has already been established in families. There are taboo subjects, which parents never talk about. As these are subjects that are never part of family conversations, the abused children are silent and their abusers rejoice and continue to make victims.

> *The culture of silence and taboos*

This book, along with our online courses, gives the ABCs of what a parent needs to address in child sex education. Each parent has a divine duty to give this education to their offspring.

Every child born is like a blank page; whatever he has on his life's page will be written down by someone. Bad advice is free and proliferated because parents who have good instructions to give to their children remain silent!

We hope, dear reader, that the contents of this book will equip you, define your language, and enable you to intentionally give sex education to your child. You will be a parent who has had a profound influence on your child's life, and he, in turn, will influence future generations.

Chapter II.

The absence of a mother

When we listen to most women recount the experience of their first menstruation, we see the absence of the parent or a mother who could give precise instructions to the child regarding this phenomenon. One lady who told us about her first menstrual period said, "I had never heard of menstruation; and my mom never taught me about it. I was playing in the backyard with my friends when suddenly they pointed out to me that I had blood on the back of my clothes. I quickly ran home to show my mother the situation, but she seemed to be ashamed asking me to go change quickly. I went to put on different clothes, then went back to play with the friends. Sometime after the same scene was repeated and I started running to my mom again, not knowing what was happening to me. She said to me, "What did I tell you? Go change quickly..."

How confusing for a child who does not understand what is happening to her and despite her efforts to seek help from her mother - who is supposed to be the person who would best help her - she is deprived of this privilege.

Many still wonder about the question of whether it is really useful to give sexual education to one's child. Yes, I think it is important, and even essential to do so.

> **For acompleteeducatio**

Sexuality occupies a central part in human life. You cannot separate a person from their sexuality; a parent cannot claim to educate their child while excluding their sexuality. Any education given to the child, without including sex education, remains incomplete.

Giving sex education to your child, makes him:

-a person who knows himself,

-a person who develops self-esteem,

-a person who is not surprised by the physiological changes of puberty,

- a person who has self-confidence, and

-a person who walks with their head held high.

Indeed, to give this education is to build the personality of the child. It is to help him understand the different unique features that he (she) has. It is a way to wake up their mind to recognize their intrinsic values and accept themselves as a unique person.

> *Building the child'spersonality*

A child who is educated about puberty, for example, will enter this period of life as a person who makes wonderful discoveries. However, one who has not had this education will go from surprise to surprise, as if life were a difficult mystery to decode. A child who has been told that at 9 or 10 years old he will have pubic or axillary hair, will be completely happy to discover these things happen to him. But for the child who has not had this education, the appearance of hair, breasts, menstruation and many other changes will fall like thunder and risks even crushing their self-esteem.

The parents' silence is an open door to sexual abuse of their children. A sexually abused child risks carrying the consequences of this heinous act for the rest of his life. Hence, parents must spare them at all costs. More than once in our lectures where we have dealt with issues of sexual abuse, we have seen

> *Effects that do not go away*

women cry bitterly for the abuse they have suffered in decades past. When they talk about it, it is with rancor and a lot of emotion as if the thing was still recent. In fact, they feel that their entire existence has been stolen from them. They have lost all self-esteem; they blame themselves over and over and wonder if it is still worth living.

Child sexual abuse is becoming more and more alarming, because on the one hand there are parents who do not want to get involved in giving this education to their children, and on the other there are those who believe that they have to do it but they are also stuck because of the lack of knowledge on how to do it.

In our approach, we say that sex education should start in the family from early childhood. It is not up to the school to do it for parents. There is no guarantee that the goal that a parent would pursue by providing sex education to their child would be the same as that pursued by other educational environments.

We know that people are also sexually abused in adulthood; in family, in schools, at university and even in professional circles. But many children, as we will talk about later in this book, are sexually abused from an early age: at three, five, nine, etc.

Every child who is born is like a blank page; everything he knows about

> **A child is like a blank page**

sexuality, he will learn, either from his parents, from school, or even from the street. However, the parents being the closest and most intimate people to the child, are in a better position to do so, and they will do so with delicacy to ensure better development of their child.

We read in the Holy Scriptures (2 Kings 13), the story of a young girl named Tamar, who was sexually abused by her half-brother Amnon, child of King David. When we read this story carefully, we discover that it is through the carelessness of the parents that young Tamar finds herself in this situation. Because it is her father, without much discernment, who sends her to go and prepare a meal for her half-brother, Amnon. Tamar was a good moral girl, a virgin, and the Bible says it was difficult for Amnon to make any attempt on her. In this story Amnon is described as a young man tormented by his sexual desires to the point that it even affected his health. He was the king's son, but he was losing weight more than anyone else, just because he was tormented

> **Emotionallytorme nted people**

by sexual desires that he could not control.

As long as there are sexually tormented people like Amnon in this world, there will always be sexual abuse. And it is up to parents to let themselves be educated, to be able to educate their children in order to put an end to this scourge.

Chapter III.

At the end of one of our lectures on sexual abuse, a lady approached me and said, "I was not going to come to your lecture as your theme was on sexual abuse, because I was never raped. I told myself that it did not concern me... But I understand that I was wrong... "

On another occasion, a young participant came to see me at the end of the conference to say: "I was sexually abused without knowing it! Thank you very much... "

All these reactions help us to understand that sometimes people push away, without knowing it, the things that should have helped them. The Bible says, *"My people perish for lack of knowledge"* (Hosea 4:6). Ignorance is not a blessing to anyone; we must fight it at all costs.

Some parents think it is inappropriate to talk about sex education. As soon as they hear the word "sex" or "sexual", they run away in advance and no longer want to hear anything. And yet in some circles, sex education is also called "family education" or "life education".

It is sad to note that everything related to sexuality remains taboo in several families. Growing up in Africa, I thought it was only in Africa that we

> **In all cultures**

did not talk about sex education in the family but living in the West today, I realize that many parents do not discuss these kinds of subjects with their children.

In several of the conferences we have held, we have understood that the majority of parents do not discuss these kinds of subjects for several reasons:

- The first and the biggest reason is 'ignorance'. This ignorance is twofold. The first is that of parents who do not know that sex education is part of the child's needs. They only care about giving food, clothing, entertainment, ensuring good academic performance, etc. The second is that of parents who know that it is a real need, but do not realize that it is their responsibility to do so. Not having received such an education themselves, they do not know that it is part of the conversations that one can have with family. They are counting on what the school does.

- The second reason is shame. Some women have told us that they don't do it out of shame. They send the children to third parties, friends for example, so that they can do it for them.
- The third reason, to name just three, is fear. Parents are afraid to approach this subject, judging themselves incapable of dealing with the child's possible questions.

When we study these three reasons, we realize that everything revolves around ignorance. Most parents are even unaware of the contents of the sexual education course that the school gives to their child which makes asking them to do it for their children seem like an impossible equation to solve.

It is God's will that every parent be equipped to properly educate their child.

What is sex education in the family?

We define sex education as *an education which opens a series of conversations between the child and the parent to help the child know his body, his development and learn how to interact with those around him* (whether in family, school or other places where the child can be found). We create a space where the parent and child can speak frankly. This education equips the child to become a well-informed, tall-walking person. To do this, the parent must know the different elements or subjects to be covered during these conversations. This will make it easier for the parent to know what to say to the child.

Even if the silence of some parents is not always an act of will; as we said above, it is time to no longer be silent. Each parent who reads this must learn through these writings to be able to initiate these conversations with their child. This book will give you the ABCs on how and what to say during this education.

Giving sex education does not mean talking exclusively about sex or intercourse. No. It is true that talking about sex or intercourse will be one of the topics to be covered during this education, but each parent must understand that *sex education is a package full of information that the child needs to receive from his parents; not from third parties, not from the street, not from school first, but from his own parents.* That is what weaves a bond of trust and deep communion between parent and child. This information will give him confidence and equip him to cope with life.

The followingchapters will help you understand what we are talking about. This information is equipment that reassures the child so that he is not surprised by physiological changes and life challenges to which the parents will already have introduced him to.

The words of a mother (or parent) are like gold; the child will remember them for the rest of his life. That's why you will even hear very old people; at the age of eighty or ninety

Mymother alwayssaid

say: "My mother always told me", "My father always told me". This makes us understand that what a parent puts in the child's heart is a lifetime investment. These are simple words, but which will remain in the child's subconscious for the rest of his life, like a rudder to guide him.

As a parent, you must not neglect your task as mother or father. It is a delicate task and a basic task. How sad it is to see a girl surprised by her first menstrual period, because her parents have never had a conversation about it. Or surprised by all the changes in puberty without the parents taking the time to converse with the child before it happens!

The parent is like a coach who introduces the child to the realities of life. This will help him to know his body, the responsibility he has for his body, and his relationships with third parties (we will discuss this in detail in the following pages). It will teach him how

> *Being introduced to the realities of life*

to behave, how to face certain challenges in life; help him understand that there are "abusive" people who can abuse his body and how he can protect himself.

I was following a girl on social media, who spoke rancorously about a family member who had sexually abused her during her childhood. And now as an adult she understands things better and I could feel the pain melt with anger when she was talking. If we go back a few years, we can ask ourselves the question of whether her mother had done her duty, that of instilling these basic concepts in her daughter, on how to protect her body or how to report an abuser. She was abused by the same person her mother sent her to be her guardian.

We said that sex education is an education that opens a series of conversations between the child and the parents; conversations

> *Do not be afraid of the term 'Sexual'*

during which the parent must help the child to know his body, his development and learn how to live with those around him. Let the parent not be afraid of the word 'sex', because sex education is also called 'life education' or 'family education.'

Chapter IV.

One lady expressed frustration when her teenage daughter looked at her in amazement and contempt while she first wanted to talk to her about menstruation. Her refusal was total, she left no opening for a conversation.

> Being ashamed to talk about it does not eliminate the reality

The parent who waits for his child to grow up and one day tells him about his sexuality will either no longer have the courage to do it, or will do it, but in the wrong way. And in most cases the child will be surprised by such a conversation which has not been part of the parent-child relationship from childhood. He will find it as interference and not a normal conversation that should exist between parent and child. This is what the parent should avoid. The sooner the conversations begin, the easier the parent's task will be.

Sex education for children should start from early childhood for several reasons. Parents should introduce certain preliminary concepts from early childhood.

If you better understand the definition of sex education that we have given here, you will understand why it has to start from early childhood.

Why should this education be given from early childhood? Here are five reasons:

1. *Because sex education is not just talking about sex or sex life.*

Sex education is a package that contains some important information for the life of the child. We should not wait for the child to grow up to jump on it and try to instill in him things that he could have learned since childhood. It is easier to educate a child than to fix an adult. From early childhood, parents have to educate the child to prepare him for how he will experience sexuality during puberty and adolescence. This statement may seem ridiculous to some, but the truth is that there are concepts that we call "preliminary concepts" that the child needs to know from the moment that he is still in the womb. These concepts become a basis on which the parent will build the pieces of the information he will give to the child. We will talk about it in later chapters.

Starting with these preliminary concepts prepares the parent and the child to deal with much more delicate subjects later on, without this seeming embarrassing or strange. In short, the child will understand that these kinds of subjects have always been part of family conversations.

2.   *Because the concept of sex or sex life and its ramifications must be approached as a logical continuation of the various conversations that the parent has already had with the child.*

Many parents who have never had these kinds of conversations with their child, often intervene in haste just to prevent, for example, the child from becoming pregnant or catching a sexually transmitted disease. Obviously, they will not do it the right way. It will either be to give condoms or expand the list of prohibited things the child should not do. A child who has been educated about his sexuality and who has developed moments of conversation with his parents will be better equipped to behave responsibly. And educating him about his sex life will not be done in a brutal way, but as a logical continuation of what they have often talked about since early childhood. This makes it easier for both the parent and the child.

3.   Because God has already prepared a natural space.

There is a natural space between 2, 3 and 5 years old, during which the child has great curiosity and asks a lot of questions. It happens to all children. When I started to study this concept of sex education in the family, I

> **Embarrassing but relevant questions**

understood that God had already prepared a natural space where parents should introduce this education effortlessly with the child.

Unfortunately, parents do not understand this. During this natural space the child is open to understanding and his curiosity is very keen. He asks questions like, "What is this? Why is this thing behaving in such a way? Do you also go to the bathroom? Why is my sister's body different from mine (speaking of the gender difference), How did the baby enter your womb? (talking to his expectant mother), how is the baby going to get out? Etc. All these questions are a good opportunity to start conversations with the child. The parent therefore has to take advantage of this space to intentionally introduce this education, in order to orient the child.

Keep in mind that everything will be done according to the age of the child, and the parent must be ready to answer anyquestions. Do not slap the child for asking embarrassing questions; rather, the parent's frank answer will give an opening for the child to ask more questions in the future. Otherwise, if the child finds that he has been fiercely criticized for his questions, simply put, it will damage the attraction of conversations he was developing with the parent. That will be difficult to restore.

For example, when a mother is pregnant, a child sometimes asks her the question: "Mom why do you have a big belly?" Calmly she will answer: "The baby is in there". For some

> **Questions thatdeserveanswer**

children, this answer will satisfy them; but others will go further to ask: How is the baby going to come out of the womb? The mother has to keep calm, she doesn't need to show the baby female genitalia, but she can tell him: "I will go to the maternity ward and we will get her out of my womb". There is also no point in lying to the child; but rather learn to give him an answer appropriate to his age, promising to speak to him in detail in the future.

4.   *The sooner a parent begins conversations, the easier it will be.*
It will be much easier for a parent who starts frank conversations from early childhood to

continue, with the child's growth, to develop more and more new topics. For example, when the child reaches puberty, the parent will be able to talk about the bodily changes that take place during this period before they happen. In fact, for such a child the appearance of pubic and axillary hair, the appearance of the breasts and menstruation, will be a wonder. And even menstruation will be expected. But the child who has not been educated will go from surprise to surprise. For a parent who has not practiced having these kinds of conversations before, starting them abruptly when there is a need will seem like a big obstacle to overcome.

5.   *Starting these conversations from early childhood benefits the parent as well as the child.* Starting sex education from early childhood not only prepares the child for the changes to come, but also prepares the parent for this great task. The child is gradually prepared to discover life, to know himself, to value his body, not to expose his nudity, to watch over his interaction with those around him, etc. This education not only educates the child, but also the parent because the latter would learn or be informed before speaking to his child, and he will also discover who their child really is.

The parent will understand that the child, even when small, thinks and can reason with his parent. After each discussion, he will go to school or to friends and come back with other questions. He will tell how he talked with his friends about the truths he learned and how he compared this with the lives of others. It's a whole school, for both the child and the parent. It's a privilege for a parent to engage in these kinds of conversations with their child; these discussions will create a place of trust that will make the child more and more open.

I often tell women during our lectures that every child who comes back from school has things to tell. The first reflex is to want to tell mom or dad, how he spent his day, what the teacher said, what the friends said, their reactions and behaviors compared to what he learned at home. What often happens is that the mom is not available, especially if she works outside the home. She returns to the family very tired and is not ready to listen and may even believe that the child is disturbing her. The child will try to relate his day each time he returns from school and if the mother continues to turn a deaf ear, he will quickly understand that it is no longer worth the trouble and his attention will turn to his toys. Let's not neglect a mother's work. Being a mother is a job that requires time and energy, especially when the children are still small.

Chapitre V.

Why do we believe that the family is the place where sex education should be given to the child?

1. Because this education must start from early childhood.

If sex education is to be given in early childhood, one thing is certain, no school or other institution will come to your home to give it to your child.

Here we give an approach according to the Holy Scriptures, according to our Christian faith. When God gave the law to his people, his law was to be passed down from generation to generation in the family, not primarily in church or school. It was in the family that we should transmit the notion of God to the child and let him know God's will on how he should live.

Let's study a little bit what Deuteronomy 6: 4-9 says:

"Hear, O Israel: The Lord our God, the Lord is one. Love the Lord your God with all your heart and with all your soul and with all your strength. These commandments that I give you today are to be on your hearts. Impress them on your children. Talk about them when you sit at home and when you walk along the road, when you lie down and when you get up. Tie them as symbols on your hands and bind them on your foreheads. Write them on the doorframes of your houses and on your gates."

By reading this text we discover that it is in the environment of the family, of everyday life that the Law of God must be transmitted, from parents to children.

First the parent must love the Lord with all his heart, with all his soul and with all his strength. As you can understand, we only give what we have. The parent is not going to pretend to push the children to love God that he himself does not love or to be devoted to God to which he himself is not devoted.

Second, the parent must keep the commandments (or the word) of God in his heart. This step is very important. Keeping the Word in your heart simply means experiencing it yourself, before sharing it with others. The parent should not be like a parrot (let me use the term), which only repeats what it has heard. He must not only know the Word, but he must also meditate on it and live it, i.e. experience its benefits so that you have the conviction and the power to transmit it to children. It's a simple concept but very effective.

Third, this transmission of the Word requires a certain technique for it to be instilled in the child. Talk about it, not once, not twice, but again and again. Repeat the same things, read, recite and sing the word, etc.

Fourth, this transmission of the Word must take place in all the circumstances of life: on waking, at bedtime, traveling, during abundance as well as during difficult times. It is therefore in this family atmosphere that God wants his Word to be transmitted to the future generation. It is in this family atmosphere that all the other concepts of life must also be transmitted, in this case Sex Education.

We said in the previous chapter that the parent should take advantage of the natural space, where the child asks all kinds of questions. To take advantage of the child's openness to engage in deep, informative and constructive conversations.

Today parents are in a hurry to send their children to daycare to pursue their careers or studies and yet if they could sacrifice even a few years to invest in the lives of their children, the happiness of the harvest would last for the rest of their lives. We should not leave the responsibility of teaching such delicate things in our children's lives to third parties. Christian parents were to be the first to give their version of "life education" to their children.

2. *Because the parent has a bond of trust with the child.*

The parent has intentions of happiness for his child. Someone who is not close to the child can claim to give him sex education, but with the aim of diverting and abusing him. There are women who did not have the courage to give sex education to their child who entered puberty for example and sent him to a friend or close family member. Unfortunately, in many cases, these people have completely diverted the child, teaching him things that were contrary to what the parents believed to be good instructions to give their child. The bond of trust between parent and child remains an important element.

In some ancient societies in Africa, it was the grandparents who gave this education to grandchildren. This did not happen in early childhood as we have seen in these lines, and there were not identical teachings to which all grandparents had to refer. Everyone did it in their own way, but all were aimed at warning the young boy or girl not to have a sex life before marriage. With the expansion of society, children born in cities and abroad, far from their grandparents, did not have the opportunity to receive this education and over time it became a thing of the past. In fact, grandparents in these modern societies do not even know that it is their duty. It is in this same logic I believe that some parents now send their children to an aunt or a friend to give them sex education.

In one of our conferences, a lady testified publicly that she trusted her sister and sent her daughter to the latter to give her sex education but to her surprise, her sister had baffled the child. And wanting to correct these falsehoods, she found herself almost in conflict with her own daughter. If a woman believes that her sister, who grew up under the same conditions as her and has received the same education as she, is the person who must give sex education to her child, this opens our eyes to understand that the problem this woman has is nothing but the shame of talking to her daughter.

Each parent must banish shame and be ready to speak frankly with their child about their body, about the changes in puberty and how to experience their sexuality. It gives a feeling of joy and great satisfaction to know that your child is being shown the way.

When I spoke to our children about the changes in puberty, each in turn, I least expected our son sometime after to come back and say: Mama, that's right! What you said happened. What a joy to see that the child is not surprised!

We were staying with a friendly family when our youngest daughter had her first period. Although warned, she was still panicking when it happened. When I found out, I had to take care of it, but one surprising thing was that in this family the arrival of the first menstruation was celebrated. Each family member came to congratulate our daughter for this new stage in her life. It was wonderful.

How much I want each little girl to be celebrated on the day she has her first period. This would give her a sense of security and an open ear for future conversations. In addition, young boys growing up in this kind of environment will have respect for girls who are surprised by their first menstruation in a classroom or in a public place.

Remember the scene I mentioned at the beginning of this book about the girl who had her first period in class when I was still in elementary school.

Dear parents, if you love your daughter, you will give her this education, so that she is prepared to face life changes with confidence and dignity.

3. *Because the subjects to be approached in sex education also depend on the goal that one wants to pursue or achieve.*

The sex education or life education that the school or the other institutions give, should not replace that which each parent had to give. For a Christian parent, his goal is to educate the child according to the word and the way of God. He will teach his child to keep himself a virgin or chaste until marriage, for example, while the other institutions will offer to protect him by using condoms. These are two completely opposite concepts. When some schools ask the child to choose whether he wants to be a boy or a girl, the Christian parent will not share this opinion. If parents give sex education while being enlightened by the Christian faith, do the other people or institutions to which the parents allow exclusivity to speak about sex education to their child, share these same convictions? Parents should not shirk their duty believing that other institutions or people will do it for them. I would like to remind parents, as we said earlier, that in some circles this education is called "family education"; it is to say that it should also be given within the family. The Christian parent will give this education by being enlightened by the Word of God.

Today's depravity among children is deplorable, which was not the case perhaps six or seven decades ago. Children as young as six, eight or ten years old have people in school whom they call 'My love'. Working also among children, sometimes I do not believe my ears, hearing children who speak without mincing their words about the romantic relationships that happen among their friends. Only parents who are naive think they should wait for children to grow up before giving them sex education or those who still hesitate to believe that it is their responsibility.

If those who give this education in some institutions trivialize the sanctity of sexuality and the respect with which it should be approached, this will always result in depravity of morals in children. This is one of the reasons why some students do not like taking the group sex education class or others disturb the class, preventing the teacher from teaching well. It is better and easier to give this education from person to person than to do it in a group. Even in family, this time of conversations should not be substituted for family reunions; these are individual moments between a parent and a child.

4. *Because education that excludes sex education is incomplete education.*

If the parent provides education for their child, not including sex education, that education will be incomplete. He will let a very vulnerable child go into the world, unable to defend himself against the insidious realities of life.

In one of the conferences we organized, we asked the participants the question of what were the things that they would have liked to learn as a family, from their mothers? The majority of these women responded that they wanted their mothers to give them sex education. Many women think they were robbed of not having mothers who could teach them the most important and intimate things in life.

How does a parent think they can educate their child well, without making them understand that managing their sexuality and relationships with third parties is an important element that can either flourish or destroy it? The parent should not only take into account the child's academic or professional success, because there are young people who have had a successful and laudatory academic and professional career but who are emotionally consumed by memories of sexual abuse.

5.   *Because many children are sexually abused in the family*

Most people who abuse others, mainly children, take advantage of a child's naivety, which is no doubt due to the fact that the parent failed to develop frank conversations with the child to educate him about his body and relationships with third parties. It can be people who live under the same roof as the child (half-brother/sister, cousin, uncle, aunt, grandparents, stepfather, guardian) or who frequently visit family (friends of parents, children of friendly families, classmates, etc.).

Because of their proximity, these people gain the trust of the child and if the child is not educated about sexual abuse, he becomes easy prey in their hands. It is not only the child who can be naive, believing that everyone around him wants good for him, parents are too. The proof is that many do not bother to equip their child with conversations, to help him understand that in this world there are also people who will try to abuse his body.

The parent should explain to the child what sexual abuse is and how these predators behave. He must show him that even people close to the family can try to abuse him, and that he has the right and the obligation to report them. For a child who is abused in conditions where the parents have never developed these kinds of conversations, it will be difficult and almost impossible for the child to confide in his parents. Firstly, because these kinds of conversations have never been part of their family life and secondly because these predators in most cases threaten their victims to never report them

Teaching a child is also building trust with the child to come to the parent with all their questions and to confide in

> **Know how to develop your child's confidence**

them when there is abuse. There are many unanswered questions in the heart of a young growing child. If this child does not open up to the parent, he will always seek to open up, because there is in him a curiosity which must be satisfied. However, he can open up to anyone at the risk of even falling into the hands of a predator. The most important things in life had to be passed on from generation to generation through clear, crisp conversations; intentionally, not on the street or with friends, but first with family.

Chapter VI.

Silence is when nobody speaks; nobody gives their point of view, when mouths are sewn shut for some unknown reason.

Silence is frightening when we know that it hides truths that no one wants to bring to the surface. Sometimes it's for fear of suffering the consequences of their acts or of being judged

> *Silence hidesfear and taboos*

by those around them; while for others, having been subjected to silence without their will, by the immensity of their disappointments or the threat of their abusers. Silence is a license that keeps those who abuse the rights of others continuing to claim new victims.

Where there is silence, taboo rules with questions that remain unanswered because we dare not ask them and they die in the silence of hearts. Silence opens the door to fear and ignorance and it can be passed on from one generation to the next.

When I think about the world we live in, I always think of it as a world that is split in two. On the one hand there is a world that I call "the world of speech". It's a world where everything is said in broad daylight. It is made up

> **A world divided in two**

of all the truths and even falsehoods that people effortlessly share. On the other hand, there is a world that I call "the world of silence". It's a world in which there are hidden truths which, willingly or unwillingly, we do not want to bring to the surface. The latter is full of everything humans want to keep secret.

In the course of my work, I have come to the conclusion that the world of silence is full of more truths than the one whose words are heard.

Most of struggles that men and women face, are internal, and for reasons that may remain secret, the majority of these struggles will hardly or never be the subject of conversation. The world of silence dictates human attitudes and behaviors. There remains an inescapable world, whose unfortunately impact on its victims deeply affects their existence.

The concept of silence in the Holy Scriptures:

In the Holy Scriptures, silence has several nuances. We will not be able to talk about all these nuances, but here are three that are most prominent:

- *In the first nuance,* silence can mean **'relying totally on God'**. Now the phrase "keep silent" simply means: wait calmly, don't be confused, trust and wait without worrying. Moses told the children of Israel: "The Lord will fight for you, and you will remain silent." Exodus 14: 13-14. In other words, the Lord will fight for you, and trust him, do not lament, do not murmur, do not be alarmed.

- *In the second nuance*, silence can mean **'humility'**. It is the obliteration of his person in total surrender to God. It is also when one avoids quarrels in front of his opponents to count on God. We observe total submission to God. The prophet Jeremiah is one of the prophets who faced fierce opposition in the exercise of his ministry. At difficult times in his life, he began to whisper and complain that God did not come to his aid. He is one of the biblical characters who suffered a lot, to the point that one of the biblical books which describe his complaints is called: "Lamentations of

Jeremiah". In the midst of his misery, when he realized that his lamentations did not change his situation, he decided to remain silent and wait for divine intervention. He says: "It is good to wait silently for help from the Lord" (Lamentations 3:26)

- *In the third nuance,*silence can mean**irresponsibility**. When one is silent in the face of a situation, when you are the voice that must defend others or that must report evil, and you choose not to do so. God addressing the Prophet Ezekiel had told him that he had made him a prophet, not to be silent, but to warn his people. If they did their duty to warn, the people would remain responsible for obeying or rejecting the message. But if Ezekiel was silent and did not warn the people, he would bear all the consequences of his silence. (Ezekiel 33: 1-9)

It is in the sense of this third nuance that we want to speak in these lines. We want to talk about the silence of this mother who could not tell her daughter that her menstruation was

> Irresponsable silence

starting soon, so the street and friends took care of it, to finally divert the attention of this young girl for the rest of her life.

-The silence of this parent who has a closed mouth to talk to his child about the changes that will happen in his body during puberty.

-The silence of this mother who herself has not received this sex education and does not know where to start.

-The silence of this girl who was sexually abused by a family member in her parents' house and who remains silent, not knowing which saint to devote herself to.

-The silence of this young boy who was expressly exposed to the nudity of his aunt and who came out destroyed in the depths of himself.

-The silence of children and other adults who are sexually abused by people who were supposed to protect them, people they trusted.

It is a world of silence, ignored by the majority of humans, but which continues to influence the attitudes and behaviors of many. Ignoring it cancels neither its existence nor its influence and who knows if it is not already living with you, or very close to you?

Talking about sex education is not a cultural matter, it is rather a divine duty.

At the beginning when the Lord put me at the heart of teaching women about sex education, I thought that African parents did not discuss this subject in family for reasons purely of a certain "African culture" but in the exercise of my work I realized that even in many other cultures of the world, parents are not very comfortable talking about this subject with their children. Even in places where people are not ashamed to kiss on the street, and in public places, many children have grown up without having received sex education from their parents.

In one of our conferences, married women and mothers from families who were asked the question *"What thing do they regret not having received from their parents or*

> **Women who regret**

that they would have liked to learn from their parents when they were growing up?" Eighty percent of them said they would have liked to have had sex education from their parents (and especially their mothers). They express it in several ways: some say that they would have liked parents to speak to them in advance about all the changes that occur during puberty. Others say they would have liked the mom to talk about menstruation, use of sanitary towels and any other care needed during this time. Others would have liked the parents, and especially the mom, to give them a preparation on life in the home, etc.

Multiple reasons behind the parents' silence.

Several reasons are at the root of the fact that parents do not give sex education to their children. Listening to women, in interviews, conferences and workshops that we organize, they often evoke the reasons that we will try to present to you in full. We will repeat the questions asked in some of our workshops and the different responses of women without modifying them:

WORKSHOPS

Questions in small groups:

1. *Name at least ten difficulties a mother encounters in providing sex education for her daughter or son?*
   - Shame or embarrassment
   - Fear
   - Lack of words
   - Taboosubjects
   - Parents' irresponsibility
   - Lack of dialogue
   - Rejection by children
   - The environment
   - Influence
   - Behavior of the child
   - The difficulty of transmitting an education that one has not received oneself.

- The culture which is not open to such a practice
- Fear of the child'sreaction
- Lack of education to give the child
- Lack of experience
- The mother's lack of education. She is not very knowledgeable and ignores her responsibilities.
- The customs or traditions of a people or a region
- Respect
- Fear of being accused of immodesty: When talking about sexuality is considered a lack of modesty
- The difficulty on how to approach this subject in relation to the age of the child
- The difficulty of knowing the right moment to approach the subject
- Shame, especially talking to a boy
- Lack of information on this subject
- Communication
- Lack of knowledge on how to approach the subject.
- Lack of time
- Because of the basic education received in the family (taboo, culture)
- Lack of an intimate relationship with the child

- Gender difference (mother - son, father-daughter)
- Parents' conflicts: there is no common discipline to help children. A climate of family tension
- Divorce of the parents: The children are straddling two houses / families.
- A delay in communication, the child has already grown
- Rely on education from school or others
- Leave the challenge to the Holy Spirit and just pray
- Frustration
- Mother'spast
- Single-parent family
- The trivialization of the subject (We do not consider it important)
- Fearing to speak early and awaking things in the child
- Not having the exact words
- The distraction of not understanding that it is our responsibility
- We imagine that the child is still small
- Because we received an education that the mother should not deal with these kinds of subjects with her child.

2. *List at least ten reasons why some women are ashamed or hesitant to talk*

about sex education topics with their children?

- The culture problem
- The environment
- Opposition between the two parents
- Lack of communication
- Lack of education or knowledge on the subject
- The atmosphere
- The child'sreaction
- Tiredness
- Ignorance
- Procrastination
- The child'smisunderstanding
- Fear
- Shame
- The tradition
- The mother is not herself a good model or example
- The difference or deviation from the intellectual level.
- Life experience (disappointment or failure in marriage)
- The atmosphere in the house
- Failure of responsibility
- The fear that the child will project this image on you
- Fear of being bombarded with questions
- A sensitive, delicatesubject

- Fear of being vulnerable as a parent
- Not finding an opportune time to talk about it
- The parent-childrelationship
- Minimize the consequences
- The fear that the child will put the advice into practice, the fear of repercussions

3.   As an adult, (and also in light of everything we learned) name at least seven things you would have liked your mother to tell you when you were little.

- The growth of a child
- How to bath (intimate bathing)
- What to do before and after sex
- The dialogue
- When, how to approach
- Speakclearly about sexuality
- How to prepare before and after marriage
- The openness and proximity between mother and child
- Talk about menstruation and physiological change
- The relationship with the opposite sex
- How to take care of your body
- How to prepare for your wedding
- Clothing

- Do not accept being touched by anyone
- Respect your body
- That mothers be open to their children from an early age
- Preparationbeforemarriage
- Training
- The testimony
- Not having had the chance yourself to discuss such matters with our parents
- Lack of openness with our parents
- Prevent consequences (negative or positive) on the sexual level
- Spend a lot more time with my mom talking about these things
- Talk about thissubjectspiritually
- Teach basic concepts (Hygiene, body changes, etc.)
- Sexual attraction to the opposite sex.
- How to take care and protect yourself
- The role of a wife and mother
- Trust me with words of love and encouragement.
- Warn that menstruation will come at a certain age
- Talk about the different phases of body change
- Talking about sex, pros and cons
- Chastity

- Attitude towards people of the opposite sex
- Warning against sexual touching (private parts)
- Do not be influenced by bad friends (in relation to their sexual experiences)
- Childbirth
- Preparation for menstruation
- Let no one touch us on the private parts
- Death
- The transformation of the body (at puberty)
- Sex, boys, friends, girlfriends, etc.

4.   What different subjects were taboo when you were growing up?
- Sexeducation in general.
- Talk about sexuality
- Everythingrelated to nudity
- The ignorance of his body
- Clothing
- Everything related to sex, marriage, talking about a friend, etc.
- The wedding
- Male   circumcision   and femalecircumcision
- Hygiene of private parts
- Pornography (exposure of our eyes)
- Lack of warning (for men)

These women are a sample, representing women from several backgrounds and

> **Break the silence !**

diverse cultures. They wrote down things they wouldn't have said out loud or in public. Deep and sad realities which they lived and which unfortunately risk being perpetuated in future generations.

Taboos reign where there is silence, where no one is raising their voices to question the taboos. Those who commit sexual abuse rejoice when their victims remain silent. Children are sexually abused in their parents' homes and their abusers are never reported because of the culture of silence.

Break the silence or stop the silence, that is when it comes to assuming our responsibilities as mother / father. Being a mother is a vocation; it is a full-time job. It's a privilege to be a woman, to know that God trusts us with great responsibility.

Breaking the silence also means preventing sexual abuse of children by committing to give them sex education (also called life education or family education). It is to be ready to answer the different questions of the children without rejecting them. Many parents do not answer their children's curious questions; they silence them and there are even some who warn them or slap them as if these were subjects that we should never talk about. Children growing up in such an environment are traumatized and will end up deducing that there are matters that should never be discussed with parents. By that time the parents will have lost them. They will open up to whoever tries to answer their questions and concerns or who wants to talk about them without asking. Remember that curiosity is part of human nature, hence it is part of the child's life too.

Breaking the silence also means making sure that subjects considered taboo are brought up in an atmosphere of listening, sharing and instruction. Bad advice is often free and is offered without being solicited, and why are those who can properly educate children hesitate and are not very intentional in sharing what they know?

Chapter VII.

The Parent-Child relationship was to be one of trust and total openness. The parent's silence on certain aspects of this relationship becomes a great obstacle to the child's development. Silence breaks the relationship of trust.

Parental silence is a language that pushes children to give them the interpretation of their choice

Even in a couple or with friends, if one remains silent and completely refuses to communicate, the other will give his silence an interpretation of his choice, by the fact that he

> *Silence speaksloudly*

cannot enter his heart to know the real reasons behind this silence. Let no parent imagine that their silence means that they did not say anything. The silence of the parent who does not want to communicate sex education to his child, is a language which makes the child believe that for the intimate things of his life, he must refer elsewhere, either to friends or to the street, but especially not with parents.

Silence speaks; it is not speechless as some believe. It speaks very loudly, except that it communicates a confused message, a bad message. Everyone has the freedom to give it the interpretation of their choice. It disorients the child in particular.

A child who has not received sex education from his mother, who has become a parent, risks doing the same to his children. It is likely that he will not do it deliberately, but as a logical consequence of his ignorance. He will perpetuate the silence. A child who has not been taught the different responsibilities he has for his body will not know from an early age how to protect himself from sexual abuse. Once abused, he will not share his disappointment with the parents (Mama); because these subjects are already taboo and we never talk about them. The child will therefore deduce that there is a certain category of subjects which are taboo, and which cannot be discussed with the parents.

Sex education received in the family will serve as a basic concept for the child, which will help him to judge any other knowledge he will acquire

> **Never deprive the child of an essential base**

later. If for the first time the child learns these concepts at school, he will always question all the instructions of the parents who will try to contradict what the school has taught him. People rarely get rid of the first concepts they believed in. Although open to learning new things, they will judge everything that comes after in the light of the concepts they had first. For this reason, the parent must do his best that the child does not start going to daycare and to third parties, without having first taught him basic concepts, which will serve him as the first concepts to which he will always have to refer.

The danger of transmitting a false Christianity.

It is sad to see that even Christian parents who are very committed to the faith raise their children in this culture of silence. They hide their lack of openness in lists of prohibitions to which they subject the child, without being able to have frank conversations with the latter. Reading the Bible every day to your child does not exempt you from giving him a sex education. It is true that it is impossible to give a balanced sex education by excluding the notion of God. This is the problem that our society has today; we want to enjoy sexuality without referring to the principles of the One who is the author. And yet for his Peugeot or Mercedes car we always refer to the manufacturer's manual. The notion of God remains a basic concept on which all education must be built. The danger of not doing this is to transmit false Christianity to your child. A Christianity full of prohibitions but which in reality does not equip the child so that he himself is able to face the realities of life. It's not for nothing that a child has a brain, it's like a computer capable of remembering instructions.

Taboos, as previously said, prevail where there is silence; where no one raises their voices to question prohibitions or report abuses. They are passed on from generation to generation blindly. In my country of origin, and mainly in my native region, there is an expression that says: "*Nsikuyabambuta*"; this term literally means "*the law of the ancestors*". This sentence is enough to silence someone who questions or opposes a practice. It is as if when dealing with the law of the ancestors one must have absolute obedience. If the first ancestors had laws, I judge them as being great ancestors and very intelligent. Unfortunately, what all the other generations after them do not understand,is that any generation that dies after these ancestors, is also classified as ancestors. And if the first ancestors had laws, managing their lives in the light of what their society was, then we, who very soon will also be counted among the ancestors, we are irresponsible for not adapting our laws to the realities of the development of our society today. They who had little light, little infrastructure, and lived in an almost closed society, knew how to have laws that managed them. Now we are copying their laws without wanting to change a comma. And even worse, these laws not being written, hence anyone who wants to use some direct or indirect power over others, will add what suits him to have subjects that will obey him.

And those who perpetuate these practices always seek to intimidate those who listen to them in the name of "the law of the ancestors." And yet everyone had to understand that he too will be an ancestor from where he must also institute new ways of doing things related to the current development of society, which will also benefit future generations.

Those who abuse others, especially children, benefit from the silence of their victims. When parents remain silent, abused children also remain silent because they know these are subjects that are never the subject of family conversations. Informing or educating the child is a way to protect him, and once abused, he will not fail to report his abuser and seek refuge with his parents.

Chapter VIII.

What is a circumcision (of a girl) ?

Circumcision is an ancient practice that involves the mutilation of the female genital organ. This odious practice affects several continents and mainly Africa; and it is generally called excision.

Excision is done in several ways, but it usually involves partial or total removal of the clitoris as well as the labia minora of the female genital organ. There are even countries where more than eighty percent of women are circumcised. It is like a norm of society, which one cannot escape.

The main reason for these practices is, supposedly to reduce the sexual appetite of women, a way it seems to protect them so that they remain virgins until marriage

> **The false reasons for circumcision**

and faithful to their husbands afterwards. Even though female circumcision is a form of discrimination against women, it is unfortunately supported by men, as wells as women. Grandmothers and mothers who practice and perpetuate it under an unconscious pressure from society. They are convinced that a girl who is not circumcised is likely to either become pregnant before marriage, to be unfaithful in her marriage or to never find a person to marry her.

Circumcision goes hand in hand with the idea of early marriage because the parents are afraid that the young girl will become pregnant, which would be a dishonor for the family. Girls, who in most cases disagree with these marriages, are taken by surprise and find themselves in the arms of a stranger with whom they are forced to spend the rest of their lives. These young girls are not allowed to say no to this forced marriage, or to wait until they are mature before they get married. They can neither dream nor decide their fate. They are victims of parents' behavior who are unable to converse with their children to transmit sex education to them. Parents who themselves have been victims of these abuses and perpetuate them effortlessly.

By the way, mothers and grandmothers who practice female circumcision act out of fear and ignorance. The fear of reprisals from a society that is rooted in these practices, and the ignorance of not knowing that there are other much more honorable and constructive ways to protect children from early pregnancies or any other depravity of morals.

Circumcision is highly encouraged by men who believe that a woman who is not circumcised will not be faithful to her husband. If the man is master of his sexual pleasure, why should the woman not be? Attempting to maim the woman to decrease her libido is a crime and besides, she will end up becoming frigid, which will be of no benefit to the man who will marry her. What pleasure would a man have in marrying a frigid woman?

Curiously in these same societies, there are parents who say no to their daughters' circumcision and who educate them to remain virgins until marriage. Whether they are a percent or two percent of the population, these parents are to serve as food for thought for the rest of the parents who do these practices.

Every mother who will allow herself to be educated by the different elements that we present in these lines and who will decide to give sex education to her child, will not regret it, and will save her children and future generations from these horrible practices which compromise development of the woman.

Consequences of circumcision

The consequences of circumcision are multiple, among other things: a circumcised woman is at risk of experiencing heavy bleeding which can lead to death or the risk of getting an infection. Some women may experience a partial closure of the vagina preventing menstrual blood from flowing normally, involuntary loss of urine, painful or torn delivery, due to scarring which no longer allows the elasticity of the vagina to facilitate exit of the baby. One-week-old babies are not spared; they are cut and risk dying of hemorrhage. Circumcised women may experience pain during sexual intercourse, an absence of sexual desires or pleasures, a lack of self-esteem, in short, a psychological conflict.

If circumcision was the solution, why are there still circumcised girls who have pregnancies before marriage?

These practices, encouraged in certain circles by most of the population, have serious consequences for their victims but unfortunately, they suffer secretly without it making the news. And yet the men who demand to marry only circumcised women, abandon those who suffer from the consequences of circumcision to go and marry others and thus continue the chain of abuse. If you continue reading this book up to the end you will be a wiser, equipped parent who will treat their children with honor and dignity.

Chapter IX.

When parents command silence to the point of encouraging matters that are totally taboo, about which you can never ask questions, it becomes an open door to abuse. Children are abused everywhere in all cultures. There are places where abuse is not reported and it goes unnoticed. People tell it to themselves in secret, and yet children suffer from it. Even children under 6 are abused without their parents' knowledge.

> Silence and taboos encourage abuse

The parent's duty is not limited to feeding, clothing, taking the child to parks, visiting certain places, or even taking them around the world. Their major duty is much deeper than just the external contribution to the child's life; it's their sacred duty to build their inner being through frank conversations.

There are parents who say: "My culture does not speak of these things". It is not a cultural problem, it is a sacred duty to which each parent must subscribe. Wherever taboo reigns, subjects that one never talks about, there also reigns confusion, sexual abuse and many perversions.

For parents who say they don't know what to say during this education, the following lines will give you the ABCs of what to say.

However, you must remember that the sex education given in one family will not be word for word identical to that given in another family. The reason is simple: the continuation of the conversations will depend on the interaction which will be made between the parent and the child and how this interaction will develop. The rest of the conversations will also depend on the child's needs and curiosity. This is what will make the atmosphere with which this subject is approached in a family to be different from the other. The depth and different topics that are

The main thing with various approaches

added on will depend on the desire to communicate that the parent and the child develop. Most of the teachings will remain the same; it's the atmosphere and the desire to communicate that will make the difference. The parent should not be afraid of the child's questions; he must be sincere in saying to the child: "I will answer you tomorrow" for example; to give yourself time to seek help from friends or elders who can help. The fear of not being able to answer the child's questions must not lead you completely to disengage from your responsibility.

A parent who wanted to talk to her teenage daughter for the first time about menstruation saw her react with astonishment and contempt, as if to say: 'What are you talking about?' 'Are you interfering in my private life'? This is why we encourage the parent to start this education from early childhood; it develops intimacy and the child will know that these are subjects that we have always talked about.

The world is very intentional about destroying the moral values of our children. Exposure to nudity and all kinds of perversions are tolerated in this modern society. However, the parents are distracted, and believe that it is the school which must give a sexual education to their children.

> *Intentionalattacks on moral values*

In fact, at school the child receives **a triple influence** that you cannot control. First the influence coming from the school as an institution, then the influence of the teacher as an individual, then the influence that each student brings from his family. Each student who comes, brings the moral or the lack of morality that comes from his family.

Even a Christian school or university does not have the power to make a big change in the morals of students. This is why we find pupils or students who seem to obey the laws of these institutions, but as soon as they are outside these radars, they get drunk, take drugs and live contrary to the principles of Christian faith. It is utopian for a parent to believe that it is the church or the school that must do this work for them.

Uncontrollable technological gadgets in our children's hands

When I was growing up around the sixties, parents were almost the only ones to teach their children. A child was in contact with the outside world only when he went to school, played with friends, or when he watched television (which many parents could not even afford). Today almost every child who is old enough to go to school has either a tablet or a smartphone. He has access to the world from his palm. It receives information in all directions that the parents are not able to control.

Even cartoons, which seem to be there just to amuse your child, give them some education. When a cartoon tells your five / six-year-old how to write a love

> *Perversions even in what seems harmless*

letter, that is sex education it gives your child while you don't even think about it. Parents and children are overwhelmed with tons of information falling out of social media every day. That's why even when they want to spend time with family, everyone has their eyes on their phone, captivated by virtual friends. The family increasingly loses not only its intimacy, but its strength and its place.

The virtual world is not without influence on the education that a parent wants to give to his child. The life of an entire generation today, if not several, is carved out of this virtual world to the point that even

> *A virtual world that takes the place of parents*

parents lose their place as educators. Video games and cartoons in certain families speak to the child more than the parents. The pursuit of a career and the fatigue that ensues make them unable to meet the real needs of the child. This is not to say that the virtual world is made up of ghosts who have absolute power over humans.

No. It is made of humans like you, but who have chosen to intrude on your privacy and impose their law on you. It is time for each parent to wake up to take control of this little land for which God has given him responsibility.

The family has the primary responsibility of educating a child, opening their minds to what is going on in the world, and showing them the way of the Lord. The church only comes second. And if parents don't, the street doesn't need their permission to make their child what they want.

Family and Taboos

Many men and women have grown up in families full of taboos; families where parent-child relationships were limited to the essentials. Families that were built in silence, i.e. families where there were no frank conversations between parents and children. These men and women who became parents today are victims of a culture of taboos and which they perpetuate effortlessly.

Parents who are unable to say to their son or daughter, "I love you", "you are beautiful / handsome". Words of simple love, but rarely spoken in family and yet used by all perverts. A child who has never heard these kinds of words in the family, as soon as someone outside tells him, he feels carried away, believing he is discovering a new world to which he is ready to give everything. The heart of any normal person is thirsty for love and he is filled when this love is expressed to him. It is in this atmosphere of love that children had to be born and grow.

Parents have their mouths shut as it pertains to their children sex education; and instead of seeking help they end up concluding that it is not their duty. Girls are surprised by the appearance of the breasts, menstruation, and whatnot. They are not taught how to wear a sanitary towel, how to treat themselves during menstruation, how to know the date of their next period, etc. There are even young girls who have gone so far as to marry, without the parents knowing that they had never had a period. What a crime!

Chapter X

The mistake that many parents make is to believe that sex education should only talk about sex, intercourse, how to prevent pregnancy, how to use a condom, in short, just about sex. This way of looking at things fills many parents with fear, because they do not feel comfortable dealing with such a subject which in several cultures is considered taboo. The parents remain silent until the

> **It is an education for life**

approach of puberty or adolescence, and when they realize all the dangers that lie in wait for the child, they begin to draw up lots of prohibitions, in a rush that can just cause the child to rebel.

Teaching the child over the years about the merits of these things is better than waiting till a certain age to make lists of do's and don'ts.

The approach we present in this book will make it easier for many parents. Before addressing anything related to sex, the parent had to give the child an essential information base to guarantee him a balanced approach to life and human relationships. The various preliminary concepts, as we have spread them out in the "list of subjects to be treated in sex education", remain an essential basis for preparing the child and the parent to converse on much more delicate subjects.

> *A balancedapproach to relationships*

It is when parents want to start this education directly with the subject of sex that things get difficult to tackle.

These first concepts help the parent to develop frank conversations with the child on important topics in life, such as the concept of God, self-esteem, the value and respect of his body, the changes of puberty, etc. And when the time comes to talk about sex or other aspects related to sex life, the landing will already be cushioned by an environment of trust, because the child will understand that it is a logical continuation of the conversations that have always been part of his relationship with the parent.

It is then that we can introduce the concept of sex and all its ramifications.

Chapter XI

The behavior of some parents shows that they have a desire to give this education to their child; unfortunately they are late in realizing the need, and they do things that in reality do not meet the real needs of the child. In most cases, these sporadic acts only reinforce the gap in relationships that already exist between the child and the parent.

1. Sex education does not mean talking exclusively about sex or sex life.

You cannot talk about sexuality without talking about God because sexuality is a gift from God and we cannot properly live it without knowing God or referring to his principles. Divine Principles remain the only user manual for living your sex life according to the Creator's thoughts. Lessons in good morals, without developing a personal relationship with God, are like a house built on sand; it only takes a minute to collapse. The child needs to be introduced to God so that he can have a personal relationship with him in his daily walk.

God is not against sexuality, as we have already said; he created sexuality so that man could enjoy it at the right time. Any child of God who wants to live a fulfilled sexuality has to know this thought of God. Some uninformed people believe that sexuality is of the devil and that Adam and Eve were kicked out of the Garden of Eden because they had sex. This reading of the Word of God is totally false and remains a devil's trick to try to twist the truth of the Holy Scriptures. In the account of Genesis, after God created man and woman, the Bible says: *"God blessed them and God said be fruitful ..."* There was no other way by which man and woman should be fruitful and if not multiply sexually. God gave them to know each other sexually. Besides, whenever the Word of God alludes to sexual intercourse, it is written: *"Adam knew his wife ..."* In chapter four of Genesis, where we find the first expression, the Bible says: *"Adam knew Eve, his wife; she conceived, and gave birth to Cain, and she said: "I have trained man with the help of the Lord". (Genesis 4:1)*

It was Adam who knew his wife; why then does Eve declare that it was with the help of God that she formed a man? Understand well Eve's reaction: she is amazed to realize that she has formed a man, but she also understands that God alone has enabled them to share their sexuality. In other words, for Eve, God is part of their sexuality. Besides, every child of God has to live his sexuality in the presence of God; i.e. taking God as a witness, praying before doing the act, and thanking him for that pleasure. If everyone lived their sexuality this way, I believe that there would never have been infidelity or fornication.

The parent who wants to give this education to his child will also introduce the notion of modesty. Show the child that we should approach this life with respect. Help him understand from early childhood that he should

> *You cannot talk about sexuality without talking about modesty*

not be naked in front of people; not get out of the shower naked; show him that he should not go to the toilet in a group with friends and undress together, that he should not enjoy watching other people's nudity, etc. These small concepts of modesty are very essential for the present and future life of the child. When these little concepts are lacking, there is no doubt that evil will settle even where we did not think about it. When the notion of sex is trivialized, it depraves morals to the point that even children under the age of ten will start talking about romantic relationships.

Today, when children are told not to be sexually active during puberty or adolescence, people are scandalized. God is right to say that sex life should be lived in marriage. Young people must learn to control themselves and develop discipline. A young person

> We cannot talk about sexuality without talking about continence

who does not know how to contain his sexual desires will be unfaithful even in his marriage. Why are so many broken hearts in our communities? Love relationships that last only a short period of time? People who cheat here and there instead of living faithfully in a marriage relationship with one partner. Is this not the result of a resignation of the parents, who did not bother to converse with their children about their sexuality!

You don't become disciplined because you're an adult; we develop this character over the years, from childhood.

The young person who wants to become a faithful husband or wife in the future, must learn to develop discipline, and to contain his sexual appetites from puberty, or adolescence. If you do not know how to discipline yourself as a teenager, it will be difficult to do so as a father or a mother. God is not stupid when he asks young people to contain themselves, and wait for marriage, to fully experience their sexuality.

Look at others as a person created in the image of God, so that one should not abuse one's body while it is developing. This person needs to grow up in soul and conscience to make the choice of the one with whom she will share her sexuality for

> *You cannot talk about sexuality without talking about respecting the other person, respecting his body*

the rest of her life, within the framework of marriage. Eros love is a jealous and possessive love, it is not shared with three or four people. If not shared only between two people, it breeds jealousy and disappointment, which if not managed well can deeply destroy those involved.

A selfish sexual desire is a desire that one cannot control; it ignores the respect and the protection of the other. It is a burning desire that is the basis of all sexual abuse that occurs in the family, in schools, at work, in universities and even in the church.

Responsible sex is only possible with respect and fear of God.

The body is like a flower. When a flower blossoms, it does not suddenly open, it takes time. Imagine that someone finds themselves in front of a flower when it is half open; if

A flower that only opens in its time

he forces its petals to see its beauty as soon as possible, he will not see its real beauty; on the contrary, it can only destroy it. It helps us understand how God created the genitals.

God did not create the genitals so that they suddenly develop, but so that gradually, over the years, they reach maturity allowing them to live their sexuality in a balanced way.

The maturity of these organs is also linked to psychological growth of the person. Just because an eleven-year-old girl has already menstruated does not mean she is ready to be sexually active. She also needs psychological development, to the point of becoming a responsible person, capable of making thoughtful choices.

Why do we say that sexual intercourse should only be experienced in the context of marriage?

This is because marriage is linked to fidelity; while for those who do it outside of marriage, these relationships often end badly. People are hurt, they think they are enemies, even to the point of wanting to hurt people they once loved. Continence today in an adolescent or young adult, prepares him to be faithful in the future.

When this sex life is lived in secret, outside the context of marriage, there are no laws to manage it and no one knows how to stop it. And yet to commit to marriage, there is a whole process to follow: teachings, guidance from society, guidance from adults and the church.

All this guidance helps the young couple to know the true value of marriage, the seriousness to put in it, and the different responsibilities attached to it.

Today there are children growing up with only one parent, because the other parent is either irresponsible, living under the parental roof, or under another roof with another woman. All this does not encourage a moral or even psychological development of the child.

Remember that this world is full of young girls who have not been able to succeed in their lives because their journey has been short-circuited by an unexpected pregnancy; fruit of irresponsible sexuality.

2.   Sex education does not mean giving your child condoms.

Many parents are unaware that educating the child is their responsibility but at a certain age of the child they realize that they must intervene to avoid a descent into hell. This is where they behave like firefighters, who only come when there is already a fire.

The parent, to whom God has given the privilege of raising a child, should not wait for times of crisis before educating their child. **A child who has been taught how to live his sexuality according to the principles of the word of God, will not need condoms**. The instruction from his parents which he received from early childhood will serve as a guide for him to make the various choices in life. It is out of fear that some parents will give condoms to their children. This is behavior that proves that we have failed in our responsibilities.

Here's what a pubescent or teenager understands when a parent gives them condoms: *"Go do what you want but protect yourself."*

Unfortunately, the parent who donates condoms believes that the only damage a child can experience is pregnancy or a sexually transmitted disease and yet the greatest destruction is not only physical but rather and above all moral and psychological...

A parent who has taken the time to provide sex education for their child from early childhood will not be ashamed to discuss any subject appropriate to the age of the child. Because he will have developed a series of conversations over the years that will allow him to make a soft landing to talk about sex life during puberty and adolescence.

This parent will teach the child how to deal with love advances from friends and others, and these conversations will become like a base, where the child will always come back to draw to orient his life.

'The world of children' is a world apart, a world where they live in realities that most parents ignore. These children being at the age of great curiosity and receptivity, they are easily influenced by films, television series, cartoons, and what friends bring to school.

> *The age of curiosity and receptivity*

For example, language such as 'having a boyfriend, or 'having a girlfriend, to signify being in a romantic relationship with a girl or boy, is a very common language even among children aged six and seven. And yet parents are naïve and believe that it is not yet time to have sex education conversations with their child.

Bombarded with tons of information

Parents are no longer the only ones influencing their child; as soon as a child starts going to school, or even daycare, they're bombarded with tons of information and behavior. If such a child has not had a family education base, which would serve as a reference, he will remain vulnerable, and at the mercy of anything.

When a child comes home from school, he often has a lot to say; it is therefore important that there is a relative at home who welcomes him and listens to him.

A earthatlistens

Every child who starts school wants to tell their parents about their day. He will do it every time he comes home from school. If the parent is still indifferent, the child will tell less and less about his day and will conclude that it is not worth it. The child, a great observer, will quickly understand that the parent is not interested in it. This is where some parents lose the closeness they had always had with their child since early childhood. Work, or the parent's livelihood should not prevent him from spending a substantial time with his child.

3. Sex education is not about just preventing a girl from becoming pregnant or preventing a child from getting a sexually transmitted disease.

Equipping the child to know about life and the dangers that await him is better than believing that you will always be close to him to protect him.

You will not always be with the child when he goes to school, when he goes on an excursion with his friends, when the friends are going to tell him things that can confuse him; when he stays overnight with friends, when a family member or someone he trusts tries to abuse him. But if the parent taught him how to protect himself; even at five he will know how to understand the difference.

Equip the child to be able to discern the dangers around him, the relationships that are good and those that are not, the attitudes of the people around him, etc. **It is better to equip the child to be awake at this point, than to believe that will always be by his side to protect him.** Even if the child is only 5 years old, as soon as he leaves the house and goes to nursery school, he is no longer in front of you at all times. Children have been sexually abused at a friend's, a relative's, a half-brother's, a cousin's, a grandparent's, an aunt's, an uncle's milieu, etc.

And even when the child is in a Christian school, the child will not be under the gaze of the teacher at all times. In addition, you will not be able to control the teacher's faith, to know whether he has faith in God or not (whether in a Christian school or not) and you will also not know what education the other children will bring from their families. It is likely that education from another family will be brought to your home through your child and vice versa. That is why the parent should not wait until the child reaches puberty or adolescence to start conversations in order to give him this education for life.

There are parents who believe that boys do not need sex education, it's girls, because they are in danger of getting pregnant. This thought is completely vulgar and false because the consequences of sexual abuse are not only physical, i.e. visible as a pregnancy. Many of the young boys who have been sexually abused have their self-esteem destroyed. They are plagued by internal conflict and even in marriage they are unable to live their sexuality in a fulfilling way.

A young boy, who cannot control his sexual desires, will not be faithful in his future home either, which for this reason can result in a divorce, with all the consequences that can cause. He may live the rest of his life separated from his children, depressed, or even plunged into drugs as a result of this lack of discipline. Every child, boy or girl, needs this education.

There is evidence today that children are most often abused by people close to the family but *if the child is educated, he will be able to distinguish and report the bad behavior of the people around him.* The consequences that follow from the lack of sex education are multiple and each parent, for the love of his child, better save him.

4.   Sex education does not mean building a bunch of prohibitions that the child must obey.

Do not wait for the child's faults to teach him. In my book called '**Woman minister in the service of the Master'**, I say that the instruction must always precede the correction. Correction takes place when there is a fault, and the parent must then recall the instruction that had already been given. The instruction is given in an atmosphere of joy and relaxation, when everyone is cheerful. Correction is done in a harsh tone, while instruction is done in a friendly and gentle tone to better communicate information. When the child commits a fault in an area for which the parent has never instructed him, he will take his time, in a gentle tone, to instruct them on the subject.

Sex education is not done through prohibitions or even taboos that can never be questioned. It takes place through very deep but also friendly conversations between the parent and the child. This education does not consist in imposing laws, but rather in making the child understand the validity of the different behaviors that he must display. These conversations will go well if the parent is also open to answering the child's questions. Many parents do not like to face their child's questions because they fear they will not have answers. Unfortunately, they fall on the defensive and take their child's questions as provocation or lack of submission. And even if that were the case, the calmness with which the parent will respond will help the child to be attentive to what is said.

A lady told me: *"I do not want kids to ask questions because I'm afraid I might be faced with questions that I don't have answers to."* I thought it was wise for a mother to think that way, but at the same time, we should not display this behavior forever. Besides, such a situation had to give the parent the desire to learn so that he was able to carry out his task. You are never born with all the knowledge on how to be a parent; we learn it. And learning to become a parent is to let yourself be instructed by what you see other parents doing, but above all by asking questions to elders who have experience and who are good role models. It is this goal that we are trying to pursue with little bit by these writings.

PART TWO

PRACTICAL TOPICS TO ADDRESS

In this part we try to list some topics to be addressed in sex education in the family but also to show in a practical way how a parent can do it effectively.

Please note that the framework of this book will not allow to cover each subject sufficiently, and that our list of subjects is neither exhaustive nor in order of importance.

If you need to know more, we encourage you to contact us personally or to consult our other publications (books, audio-visual, digital or online media — as displayed at the end of this book).

Chapter XII

The first concepts

The parent must devote his time to the education of his child. If he does not give enough of his time today to educate him, he will be caught up in the near future by the consequences of his silence. I advise women to invest their time in children when they are little because at a certain age, although living under their shelter, children will cease to depend entirely on parents. They will be able to search for the information themselves and especially if the first concepts to channel it in life they did not receive it from the parent, then everything the parent tell them will be assessedbase on what they previously heard elsewhere. The first concepts that the child receives are very essential because they will become a base, on which he will always evaluate all future information. It is preferable that the parent be the channel through which the child receives these first concepts of life.

Sex education is not just about sex; it talks about everything the child needs to know to train their physical, moral and emotional person. This information is carefully placed one after the other according to the age of the child.

Giving the child sex education does not mean stuffing them with rules of

> *Create a relationship of trust*

what to do and what not to do. Rather, it is about creating a relationship of trust that allows the child to receive instruction, ask questions and share thoughts, without being hypocritical. You know, the attitude of some parents made their child hypocritical without them knowing it. If a parent is open, the child can fearlessly share what they think and ask questions for the purpose of instruction.

The atmosphere that will surround these times of sharing between parent and child will determine the quality of the interviews that will follow. These interviews must take place in an atmosphere of joy; the parent must show great mastery in the face of the child's possible reactions and questions (especially for children who have never been spoken to until an older age.) Avoid this time of conversations becoming a moment where one parent speaks to give orders. The child also needs to reassure himself that if he shares his thoughts, they will not be the object of blame, but rather of reflection. And if the parent has a contrary opinion, he will pass it on firmly, but without anger, explaining its merits.

The different topics to be covered in sex education depend on the environment.

Withfamily, school, church, ...

When we speak from one environment to another, we want to refer more to the family, school, church, or other organizations that educate children. It is true that in several circles this education is given in school but in God's mind , it should be done first in the family, from early childhood. This is to join what the Bible says: *"Teach the child the way he should go and when he is old he will not turn from it"* *(Proverbs 22: 6)*

The alarming statistics of sexual abuse of children, adolescents and young adults are an urgent appeal to parents to say: 'Children should be taught as a family so that they are equipped to face the realities of life'. The fact that a child has never been spoken of sexual abuse does not mean that it never happened to him; he may just be another victim of this culture of silence. Our societies are filled with children, young people and adults who are victims of sexual abuse, who are unhappy with their parents because they blame them for not having sufficiently protected them but like their parents, they too remain silent and will never speak to them about it.

Christian parent

The sex education that is taught in school can have many similarities to what a Christian parent would teach but if the things taught by the school are contrary to the Christian faith, the Christian parent would not accept them. When children in kindergarten are already asked to choose whether they want to be boys or girls, this is completely contrary to the word of God and the notion of self-esteem that parents have to teach their children. The parent, on the contrary, will say to his child: "You were born a girl, God wanted it so and you must be proud of who you are", "You were born a boy, God wanted it so, and you must be proud of being a boy".

This helps each parent to understand that the topics we are talking about may be the same as the ones the school is about, but the concept that we want to convey to our children as Christian parents is not necessarily the same with the school. Even if different families tackle the same topics, the development of conversations will be different from one family to another; because where the child asks questions the conversations will be much deeper than where the child is just an observer. And where the parent is open to answering the child's questions, the conversations will take on a much more cheerful trend than where the parent would be frozen.

Here is a detailed list of the different topics that a parent can discuss to provide sex education for their child. We will list those that are most essential and each of the subjects will be dissected in the following to make it easier for parents:
- Preliminaries (the notion of God)
- Prayer
- The concepts of politeness (respect for parents, elders and others)
- Know and take care of your body
- Self-esteem
- Respect for your body and others
- Nudity (pornography)
- The danger of seeing the nudity of others
- The parts of your body that no one should touch

- Sexual abuse
- Sexually abusive people
- Changes in puberty
- Friendships
- Virginity
- Sexual intercourse

Chapter XIII

1. The vertical relationship

The notion of God is the basis of any education that a Christian parent would like to give to his child. It's the foundation on which to build the child's life. You cannot believe in raising well your child without teaching him the concept of God. We introduce this notion from early childhood, by small gestures: When you pray before sharing the meal, before sleeping or with the child before putting him to bed, on waking, say thank you to the Lord, pray for your needs, etc. These acts may seem trivial, but they are effective in introducing the concept of God even to a baby a few months old. Of course, the child will not have visible reactions since he is still only a baby... But these concepts will take place in his subconscious until the day when he has a full understanding.

Introduce God as a heavenly father, introduce the concept of prayer, the concept of God as one who sees everything, even actions done in secret, and also as an emergency aid. The child will eventually understand that there is a supreme being, whom we do not see, but who is there, who exists, with whom we speak, who listens to us and answers our prayers. As the child grows, he will understand that these prayers are not empty gestures, God hears them and answers them.

The parent has the first responsibility to introduce this notion of the vertical relationship to his child. It is a mistake to believe that it is up to the church to do so. It is a concept that had to be learned in the first months and years after the child is born; i.e. within the family. In church or Sunday school, the child has to receive confirmation of the things he already learned in family. The parent should not shirk his duty; the first church of a child is the family; it is the home of his parents.

Since ancient times, the law of God has been passed down from generation to generation within the family. The parent had a duty to instill the law of God in their child and in generations to come. This text from Deuteronomy 6: 5-9 gives us a very clear and precise message on this subject.:

"And these commandments, which I give you today, will be in your heart. You will teach them to your children, and you will talk about them when you are in your house, when you go on a trip, when you go to bed and when you get up."

There is an important truth in this text, to which I would like to draw the attention of each parent; God says, *"These commandments... will be in your heart."* The parent himself must first have the faith and the Word of God in

> **We only give what we have**

him, in his heart; because you only give what you have. If the parent himself does not believe and does not know the Word of God, he will be unable to transmit the concepts of the vertical relationship to his child.

There has always been a natural intimacy, especially between mother and child. It develops during the months of gestation, the hours of breastfeeding and the various treatments that the mother administers to her baby. Many mothers unfortunately limit themselves at this preliminary stage. When the time comes for them to introduce much more delicate subjects, they resign. And yet it is also the time when the parents' coaching is most needed by the child.

2.   *Talk to him about his body*

The notion of cleanliness is like the second notion the parent will have to introduce to the child. It seems simple but it will establish a truth in the child, who will understand from an early age that parents have great knowledge and that with them he will always have things to learn: brushing teeth, washing hands before and after each meal, washing hands after using the toilet, wearing clean clothes after showering, combing hair, etc.

It is the easiest way to introduce sex education. It's a starting point to make him understand the why of certain things that have been done to him regularly so far, and how he can do it himself. For example: why we wash, why we brush our teeth, why we wipe our behind after going to the toilet, why we do not go out of the bathroom naked, etc. The parent will not act while keeping his mouth closed because this early instruction will help the parent and child get used to these kinds of conversations. This will also allow the parent to introduce more delicate subjects in respect to the age of the child.

In this notion of cleanliness, talk to him about the consequences of eating with dirty

> *A healthy mind in a healthy body*

hands, not brushing his teeth and many others. It is also a way to introduce a lesson on the different parts of his body: The head, the eyes, the nose, the ears, the mouth, the teeth, the tongue, the breasts, the belly, the genitals, the thighs, the knees, the armpits, the fingers, etc. You do not have to be a biology or anatomy teacher to tell your child that the eyes help to see, the mouth helps to eat, to express yourself, to sing, to praise God, etc. It sounds like a joke but this almost fun time is crucial to seal the opening of conversations between mother (father) and child. This prepares you to tackle much more delicate topics in the future.

These different concepts are not subjects to be dealt within a day, a week or at one time. No. These things will be taken on by the parent over and over for years. The parent needs to give time to educate their child. A mother's task is a long-term job; a full-time job. I urge mothers not to shirk their duty because in the future the consequences may be difficult, if not impossible to correct. Rest assured that the child receives from you the first concepts that will serve him as basic concepts which he will use to assess any future knowledge.

3. Respect and protection of his body

The notion of respect for one's body is also closely linked to the notion of the protection of one's body and the relationship with third parties. The instruction the child will receive at this point will also equip him to protect himself from sexual abuse.

Help the child understand that his body is a gift he has received from God and for which he / she will be accountable. Showing him that his body is a wealth, it is the first capital that God gives him and that he will have to invest for the rest of his life. Help the child understand that God has put gifts and talents in him that he can use to make a living. This is why we said that sex education is not there to talk exclusively about sex; rather, it is a bundle of information from parents the child needs to learn. It's building and guiding the life of a child. The child on his side will more and more discover that his parents are geniuses and will remain thirsty to learn new things from them. Also help the child understand that his body is a property that he has the primary responsibility for caring for and protecting.

At this moment the child is growing, the parent must become more and more specific: he will tell him that there are not only good people in the world and that there are also bad ones who can abuse his body. Imagine a five-year-old child who returns from school and tells his parents that another child has touched his 'penis' (genital organ) ... What would have happened if this little child had not been educated on protection of his body?

To tell the child without reservation that there are in this world, and perhaps even in his immediate entourage, ill-intentioned people, who have bad intentions and who can abuse his body. This way of educating him is also a way of protecting him.

Define in language that a child can understand, what is a good person and what is a bad person. Do not transmit unnecessary suspicion and hatred to the child, no. If you are in conflict with or dislike some people, be careful not to pass this hatred on to the child. Rather educate him in the light of the Holy Scriptures to protect his body and report abuse. Many children unfortunately are naive and because of the parents' silence, they think that everyone close to the family has good intentions concerning them; and yet most children are abused by these same people close to the family (aunt, uncle, cousin, half-brother, half-sister, family friend, friend, grandparents, etc.)

Teach the child, for example, that there are parts of their body that no one should see, touch, or kiss (the chest, genitals, buttocks, thighs, stomach, ears, the navel, mouth or any other part of the body which would violate his privacy or will.)

Show the child that if someone pushes their mouth into theirs to kiss them, that person has no good intentions towards them.

Teach the child to report anyone who tries to indulge in touching parts of their body. Many children do not report people who have sexually abused them because they have not been educated to do so. Show the child that they have a duty not only to protect their body, but also to report anyone who wants to abuse it. All those who sexually abuse children threaten them so that they do not report them. Since most children live in fear of reporting their abusers, only the instruction of the parent can break this fear and reassure the child that he can report it and be safe. These abusers use language like: "If you talk about what we did here, I will kill your father", "If you dare to talk about it nobody will believe you", "If you don't talk about it, I will give you gifts", "If you talk about it, your parents will fight and may even separate", etc. A child who finds himself faced with these kinds of threats, will not be able to get out quickly unless the parents have had the time to educate him on this danger.

Failure to tell the child that there are malicious people who can abuse his body is a serious mistake, which leaves him vulnerable. From the age of four, the parent will help the child to know the different parts of his body that no one should touch.

Chapter XIV

Decades ago, parents could not imagine that their children would be exposed to pornography. Nothing could foresee it because all outside influence was through television, school or friends, to name a few. Today pornography is within everyone's reach even where we do not want it, and the kids are not spared.

A real invasion

Some parents think that to talk about this subject is to arouse the child's curiosity; they ignore that infants are exposed to tons of information. Children almost have television setson their hands (telephones). If your child doesn't have a phone, you don't know if their friend at school has one, and they may still be exposed to things you cannot control.

We do not want to tell you here that you're going to tell the child everything about pornography, no. First, you are going to instruct the child not to expose their nudity and not to look at that of others. These two concepts alone are of paramount importance for the child's life; if the child can live with it, it will already save him from falling into this trap of trivializing nudity and its consequences. He will know right away that watching pornographic images on television, on the computer, on the phone, or on some other media is not acceptable.

Apart from this nudity which is conveyed by the media (social or not), there are also malicious people who expose their nudity to children or who undress children to see their nudity. People who take advantage of their position to touch children or people who cannot defend themselves. An adult for example who stays naked in his room, but calls a child to give him this or that other thing... An adult who takes advantage of a moment when he is alone at home with a niece, cousin, half-sister or brother, to be naked and go about his business as if nothing is happening. These practices and many others are also done by children who have been abused in the past and who in turn touch their little sisters, little brothers, and cousins.

The parent will dress his child in decency from an early age. If the girl learns at a young age not to expose her chest or her thighs,

> *It all starts in childhood*

she will keep this good moral even in adulthood. Otherwise if we dressed the child as we would a doll, regardless of modesty, when this child grows up and we ask them to change their way of dressing for reasons of modesty, they will not understand why. And I will totally agree with such a girl because she assumed that everything the parents had allowed in her life was morally correct and good for her. It is up to the parents to show the child the right path from early childhood and not to play with their responsibility. If at six they put on a panty that shows the tips of her buttocks, don't get angry as a parent that she wears the same kinds of panties at eighteen or even being a mother. It makes sense doesn't it? She just replicates the model she was taught.

Dangers for those who do not report their abuser

Anyone who does not report their abuser has two dangers that await them: Either he becomes an abuser himself, who will abuse others, or he now considers himself a useless and worthless person. Reporting his abuser is very important: on the one hand, it boosts the victim's morale, namely that he knew how to defend himself, and on the other hand, it will prevent him from making new victims. In fact, a person who reports his abuser triumphs over him and sets out on the road to restoration.

Teach the child for example that he should always cover himself after his shower and not go out naked to cross the corridor or even run to the living room where his brothers are. He may not understand everything, but at least he will grow up with a sense of respect for his body. The Word of God has a whole chapter where God asks his children not to expose their nakedness or to see that of others. (Leviticus chapter 18).

Parents themselves should be role models for their child, and not ask them for things that they themselves do not obey. I was in a children's meeting, I was teaching that it was not good to look at pornographic images, when a child of ten years raised his hand to say: 'But why then the parents watch! 'I was red with embarrassment; however, I gathered my courage to answer him. The parent should not have a double life; children are great observers. Do not teach them a moral to which you yourself do not subscribe.

Today pornographic images are shared like hotcakes in social media and many children are victims. When respect for nudity is trivialized, there is always a danger of depravity in children but the teachings of parents will serve as a safeguard.

This conversation on nudity will also help the parent to introduce the concept of sexual abuse a few years later.

Chapter XV

The human being is an impressionable being. All that he becomes is the fruit of the influence he undergoes throughout his life. What he sees and what he hears has a great influence on him. Parent should

A
veryimpressionablebei

instruct the child to watch what he sees and hears. It is sad to see that when a child grows up in the midst of adults who speak profanity, the child will also grow up with this way of doing things.

As a parent you must also have good friends; because it is possible that their children will leave some influence on yours. You don't choose your biological brothers; but friends are your choice. If they have a bad influence on your family, it's your choice.

Several decades before, parents had total control over the information to which their children were exposed but today it's almost impossible. Children are exposed to tons of information, unbeknownst to parents. And even cartoons that a parent would believe a good option for their child, unfortunately contain compromising information, contrary to the good education that the parent wants for his child.

Teach the child to be the one who influences others with good, instead of being badly influenced by others. Tell the child that their friends need to hear

> *Know how to influence instead of being influenced*

the good things they learn at home. This will motivate him to intentionally be the one who influences others.

Each parent who exposes children to a film or cartoons, had to watch it themselves to judge the content before putting it within the reach of children. I decided one day to watch a film (cartoons), just out of curiosity, and to my surprise these cartoons were discussing: 'how to write a love letter'. I was surprised to see that such a topic could interest children. In reality a child who watches such a cartoon will automatically believe that "the love letter" is something that children of his age must also do. Why? Because like those who talk about it use children's voices, the child not knowing that these cartoons are designed by adults, probably thinks that these are things that other children of their age do; hence he too will want to do it. Unless banned, children do what they see adults or other children do.

Many children are destroyed at a young age, because the parents are often too busy to pursue their careers or their studies and parental supervision is almost nonexistent. Every child who comes home from school has things to tell but there is a danger when the parent does not listen to him. The child will continue to do so, but over time their desire to tell the story will fade away because the parent is not interested in engaging in conversation. The little child can tell you everything that caught his or her attention at school, whether positive or negative. It is up to the parent to take the opportunity to start constructive conversations and seal this opening of conversations between parent and child. It is not a masterful time when you make him sit down to say: "Go on, tell us what happened in school today?" No. It must be done in a relaxed atmosphere where the child freely tells his day and understands that you are listening to him. This must be done first in response to his need to communicate and to check how he is putting into practice the things that are taught to him at home. Teach the child to know what is good from what is bad, and not to be influenced by evil.

Children do not stay longer with parents. At twenty, if they have not yet left the parental home for university; they are already preparing to leave. The time invested by parents in their lives will never be in vain; it will bear fruit for the rest of their lives and they will be forever grateful. It is up to the parent to sacrifice his time and efforts during the first years of the child's life to secure a peaceful future.

Better educate a child than correct an adult.

Chapter XVI

Self-acceptance

Everyone that God created is a wonderful creature. The parent needs to help the child accept himself, to believe that he is beautiful, that she is beautiful; to believe that God put him into this world to do things that only he can do. A child can be born with these predispositions, but the greatest work to reassure it must be done by the parent. A child can be

Help your child know how to assert himself

beautiful, brave and intelligent but at the same time lack self-esteem. It is up to the parent to build this inner person with words of appreciation, encouragement and love.

The lives of many children are destroyed because they do not esteem themselves; they live in a toxic environment, where we only notice what is negative in them and never their strengths. You never appreciate what they are, except that you point the finger at what they cannot bring to the table. Children put down and insulted all day long by parents or guardians who do not assess the seriousness of their words.

The parent is not an observer of the child's life, to see how he will manage; no, he is the architect. It is up to him to help the child understand that he is an important person, that he is very valuable in the eyes of God, that he is unique and created in the image of God. I really like a text from the Holy Scriptures that every parent should know and read to their child:

Psalm 139: 13-14 *"It was you who formed my innermost being, who wove me in my mother's womb. I praise you for being such a wonderful creature. Your works are admirable, and my soul recognizes this well."*

It is extremely helpful if a parent says to their child, *"I love*

> **The strength of words of love**

you my daughter" or "I love you my son." Words of love have strength; they comfort, uplift and reassure the person who hears them.

There are no cultures in the world where you don't show love for each other. It is to show love that people kiss when they meet; it is to show love that they say hello in one way or another. Beautiful words, words of love or words that appreciate others, leave no one indifferent. The heart of every human becomes tender before such words and every child needs them. A girl who has never heard her father say "I love you" will easily fall into the trap of any man who tries to tell her.

Make your daughter understand that she is beautiful and that her beauty is not the result of a contest or competition, makeup, group acceptance, or compliment. Help her understand that her beauty is of intrinsic value, a feature that makes her unique. A child who does not value himself is not sure of himself. He will never believe in what he is or what he can do without the approval of others.

The child's environment and the words the child hears as they grow up have a big

> **A**
> *destroyedidenti*

influence on them. A child who has always been told that he has big eyes, a big head and what do they know, will grow up for the rest of his life with the thought that he is not beautiful and will be difficult to accept.

It reminds me of the story of a young man who always had a very special hairstyle. To my question of why he did his hair like that; he made me realize that there was a whole story behind this hairstyle. He replied, "I am doing my hair like this to hide my ears." I was curious to know why he had to hide his ears. Then he will say to me, "Because since childhood I had always been told that I had long ears..." I was very touched to hear this confession, especially to see that this young man was an intellectual. All the knowledge he had accumulated at the university did not erase the little words that were said to him in his family when he was very young. This is how negative words this young man heard from childhood continued to erode his self-esteem.

It is difficult to appreciate others, or even your own child when you do not accept yourself. It is easy to project onto others the lack of self-acceptance. We look at others

> **The venom of contempt**

against what we think they don't have, instead of appreciating what they have. The parent must learn to accept himself first, lest he vomit this venom of contempt on others, including his offspring.

The difference is like night and day, between a child who comes from a family where he has been looked down upon, and one who comes from a family where he has been valued. When one will always have to complain, the other will have a language of victory, when one will believe that life is full of insurmountable obstacles, the other will find in these obstacles opportunities to shine.

Developing a child's self-esteem also means helping them to discover their potential, to believe that they are capable and to help them face life with determination. If you do this, the child will remain

> *Help your child discover his potential*

grateful for the rest of his life, because he will understand that the parents were great coaches, who introduced him to the realities of life and put him on the right track.

Chapter XVII

As the conversations continue, the child is growing. Right now, the child is approaching eight and the parent is preparing to talk about puberty. The parent is not going to wait until the child is already going through puberty before telling them about the changes that happen during puberty. By the end of his first seven years the child already has a capacity to understand things well and the parent can start conversations about puberty changes at the age of eight. For parents who find it difficult to provide this education, birthdays are also great opportunities to start some of these conversations.

A lady asked me if it was not very early to talk about these changes at the age of eight; she was afraid of giving the child too much information. And yet another lady who waited until the child was nine, during the conversation when the mother was trying to take turns to bring up the real subject, her daughter understood right away, and she asked the question: "Mom, what are you talking about, the period?" The mother could not believe it; she only realized that the child had already learned it elsewhere. Remember we said that there is an advantage for the parent to be the first person to discuss these kinds of topics with the child. In children, the information that arrives first becomes like a database which will be used to judge any other future information.

This is not an anatomy lesson that the parent will give to the child, but simple

> *This is life, not an anatomy class*

information on the changes that will happen to his body in the years that follow, so that he will not be surprised.

A lady told how her daughter with whom she had not yet had conversations came to see her father to say: "Dad look, I have hairs growing under my armpit..." backwards? Instead of the parent being the one who should inform the child about these changes in puberty, it is rather the child who, surprised, comes to announce it.

Talk about these changes with enthusiasm; as good signs in the stages of growth.

For example, say to the child, "You are entering a wonderful stage in your life now that will make you a great person. This stage of life will be characterized by changes that will happen in your body. In the following months or years:

A wonderful stage

- You will notice a growth of the hairs under the armpits and on the pubis (to the boy as well as to the girl).
- Your breasts will start to grow (to the girl)
- "One day you will have what is called" menstruation" (to the girl). Did you know that?

Talking about menstruation and how to go about it

It just means that one day you will see blood on your panties, or when you go to the bathroom; so don't panic, it is menstruation. All the women in the world go through this. It is a sign that you are growing. If this happens when you are at home, run quickly tell me and we will congratulate you; but if it happens while you are at a friend's or at school, I will show you what you are going to do."

Show the child a sanitary towel and how it can be used.

In some circles, a sanitary towel is not a luxury. Just as we have toilet paper in public toilets, we also have sanitary towels as an emergency kit for women. Just as you provided diapers at the birth of your baby, so you must provide sanitary towels to your daughter who enters puberty.

- Teach the child how to take care of herself during menstruation:
- Examine the different kinds of sanitary towels and choose the ones that are a good option for your daughter.
- Show the child how to dispose of an already used towel before putting it in the trash.

These concepts may seem basic, but they will help the child's life.

Towels, towels and towels

During a youth camp, I went to the toilet and in the trash was spread across its entire length and width, a towel full of blood. Not only were the toilets common to girls and boys, but no matter if you were a boy or a girl, no one could sit back and not react in front of such a towel. It is disgusting.

Here's what to do:
- The towel already used can be rolled up on itself and the glue which is below the towel will allow the latter to close on itself. Once rolled up, you can pass toilet paper over it and put it carefully in the trash.
- Help the girl understand that she needs to change regularly; do not keep a towel for more than four hours. Also, do not change too frequently especially if it is a tampon, to avoid damaging the vaginal mucosa.
  - The girl should immediately wash any sheet or clothes accidentally tainted by her period.
- Overflow can be avoided by choosing towels with wings. These wings help the towel stay in place regardless of movement.

- There are also washable sanitary towels, that is, towels that you can wash after use and reuse.
     Often the temptation is to believe that everything that is for single use is modern and better. Think again. Washable sanitary towels are modern and available on the market. They have many advantages that you should not ignore: They are very comfortable, once you attach the clip located at the end of the wings to the bottom of the panties, they do not move. They have no chemical components, they are

economical, and they can be reusable for several years.

For those who live in environments where single-use sanitary towels are not available, there is nothing to regret; either you buy washable sanitary towels or you make them yourself.

- Washable sanitary towels require great care. Once removed, run the towel over with water, then clean it with soap and dry it. If you do not tumble dry, iron it before another use; it is a way to sterilize it. Be careful not to clean your towel with hot water, otherwise the blood may stick to the cloth. A towel that holds smells after a few uses must automatically be put in the trash; but in general, these towels can be reused for a long time without leaving any odor.

- Every mother will take her time to explain all these little things to her child. Isnot this sex education or life education! Gradually introduce your child to the realities of life.

The wearing of "pads" is the subject of much controversy in several circles. Especially in cultures that encourage virginity before marriage and those who believe that wearing tampons breaks the hymen, which is a small membrane about one centimeter from the entrance to the vagina and is considered proof of virginity. We believe that virginity is very important for young people who are preparing for marriage; that is why we talk about it in the next chapter but before that we want to note some ambiguities in relation to the hymen:

It is true that the rupture of the hymen remains as a sign of virginity during the first sexual intercourse and is noticed by a slight bleeding. But it is also important to understand that a significant number of virgin girls do not bleed during their first sexual intercourse. The hymen can break outside of sexual intercourse, for example during physical exercise. Hence the absence of blood during the first sexual intercourse does not necessarily mean the absence of virginity. Just as the presence of blood does not necessarily mean that the person is a virgin. Today there is an artificial hymen in the form of a capsule, which a woman can insert into her vagina during the wedding night to give the impression of virginity.

However, for cultural reasons or for the pride and personal safety of the girl in relation to her marriage, we encourage the use of sanitary towels which is much simpler and more universal.

Talk enthusiastically about all these bodily changes at puberty. Present them as good signs in the

Talk about it with enthusiasm and modesty

stages of the child's growth: the appearance of breasts, pubic and axillary hair, menstruation, attraction to people of the opposite sex, etc.

In boys, puberty takes place between 11 and 14 years of age, while in girls it is much earlier, from the age of 9 onwards.

As a parent, you are not there to tell the child about the negative effects of puberty on their temper. For example, a parent who says to his child: "Well, during puberty you will have mood swings, feelings of rebellion, but these are the effects of hormones in you, so you have to overcome them". No. This is not your role ... This information is used by you to get to know your child's psychological state, so that you can be patient with him while he is going through a teenage crisis, for example. But if you stuff his head with information about these hormonal effects, every time you blame him for his behavior, he will say, "You know, it is not me, it is the hormones in me."

One of the great psychological changes in puberty is the birth of sexual desires. Explain to the child, for example, that the attraction he may feel for people of the opposite sex is normal, except that he must know how to channel his feelings and control his desires (We will talk about this in the following chapters). Today children, especially those who are already in school, talk about love life even in primary school. So, it is a fault for a parent to be hesitant and not to tell his child that the erotic life is not for children but for married people or those preparing for marriage.

Chapter XVIII

Do not think that to give sexual education to the child is to give him condoms. The notion of relationships with people of the opposite sex can be introduced smoothly, if these conversations start at a young age.

Virginity is an important stage in the child's life; it trains him to manage his sexual desires. If every sexual desire is to be satisfied immediately, then no one in the world would be faithful to his partner. Humans would become like wild beasts.

> **Know how to manage your desires and stay pure**

It is also because people do not control their sexual desires that there is sexual abuse: A parent who abuses his child, a brother who abuses his sister, a friend who abuses his friend, an uncle, family friend, etc. Puberty and adolescence are a time when God wants every young person to practice a pure life.

Anyone with whom one lives sexually leaves a life in the life of the other difficult to erase. This is why the Bible says that any other sin that a man commits is outside his body, but he who sexually lives in disorder sins against his own body. Some households are in difficulty for the simple reason that spouses live their sexuality based on past experiences.

Repeat in the ears of the child, that the will of God is that every boy and girl marry virgins, without having had sexual intercourse with anyone. This is what symbolizes the white attire that brides put on to receive

> **Snow white, body and soul**

the nuptial blessing. You know, this is a great time for engaged couples who come to receive the nuptial blessing without their having known each other sexually; while for those who have already had sex, the white attire and even the ceremony of the nuptial blessing becomes meaningless.

It is not the parent's duty to follow the child wherever he goes to watch him; rather teach it so that it understands the merits of this abstinence and that it lives it without constraint.

At the time when it is believed that the youth of today are corrupt, and that all lead an active sex life, there are thousands of young people who live in abstinence and marry virgins (boys and girls). By the way, abstinence is not a deprivation; it is a discipline for a fulfilling sexuality.

In some circles, virginity is understood to be the imposition of men on women. It is like a form of domination of the man who wants to appropriate the woman as his private good.

This is an opinion that I do not share at all. These people need to understand that virginity in the Christian faith is not only required of women. Both men and women are called to remain virgins until marriage. If the woman does not want to belong to one man, then will she love a man by wanting to share him with several other women? If a man does not want to belong to one woman, then will he love a woman by wanting to share her with several other men? Marriage has never been established for three or more people. It is an exclusively two-person relationship; the man and the woman.

If virginity was of less importance, women would not seek plastic surgery to restore their hymen. Instead of seeking an artificial virginity, natural virginity remains the only reassuring way, for a fulfilled and satisfying sex life.

Surgery to regain your virginity ?

Keeping your virginity is not only dignified and honorable, but it is just as possible and easy as staying faithful in your marriage. Anyone who resists the temptation to lose their virginity before their marriage will have control over the temptation to cheat in their marriage because this is first a matter of the heart and not just the management of one's desires.

Chapter XIX

The lives of many children are short-circuited by an active sex life, when they should have enjoyed their adolescence and their virginity. The parent has a duty to help the child understand that virginity is not a state of weakness or dishonor, but an important stage which he must enjoy, and which prepares him for a life of discipline and mastery in what concerns sexuality.

The parent should be relaxed and ready to answer questions from the child. If you donot have an answer, promise to answer it soon and in the meantime, get educated on the

Several questions about sexuality

subject or ask elders who can help. Help the child understand that intercourse is not child's play, but that he will enjoy it fully in marriage.

The child needs to know that any adolescent girl who loses her virginity regrets it. One girl said with regret that she had sex with a boy, and after the act when the boy realized she was a virgin, he said to the girl, "Forgive me; I did not know you were a virgin." If ahorny boy understood that virginity has a price, how much should that awaken the attention of young boys and girls to keep themselves pure! Early sex life can have many drawbacks on future life in marriage.

Also tell the child that a girl who loses her virginity can become jealous of those who are still virgins, to the point of pushing them in one way or another to live in relationships that will lead them to lose too their virginity.

Talk to the child about the consequences of an early sex life and be prepared to answer all their questions in a calm and informative manner.

The parent will be careful not to encourage an active sex life with young adolescents because all the erotic relationships of the past will leave a history which in the future can negatively affect the relationship in a home.

Educate the child to understand that the relationship with a person of the opposite sex does not always have to be an erotic relationship. One should not always love with a desire to live sexually with the person.

For the child who is preparing for marriage, the parent will generally speak to him about the behaviors he believes useful in solidifying the life of a couple. Both boys and girls need this support. Young people preparing for marriage do not need to be shown how to have sex. Even an animal believed to have little intelligence knows how to have sex as soon as it is old enough to be in heat.

Prepareyourchild for marriage

The sex life of a couple must be unique, the fruit of an experience discovered by two, and not a copy of what we have heard or seen on pornographic images. A couple who build their sex lives on models seen elsewhere are doomed to failure.

The parent will give the child all the advice relating to fidelity, communion in the home, respect for the other, care before and after intercourse, etc. But in the actual sexual act, the couple will have enough instinct to have a unique experience.

Today even children under the age of ten have erotic affinities between boys and girls; something some parents do not realize yet. Cartoons and other media tell children about erotic life without parents realizing it.

> Consequences of
> an early sex life

The parent's life education conversations with the child will help them understand that there are serious consequences that can happen if you do not know how to control your sexual desires.

Here are some consequences that can happen when young children get into a sex life before marriage:

1. Loss of virginity (often in insecure conditions)
2. A life of cheating and hypocrisy that we can never stop
3. A rebellionagainstGod
4. Sexually transmitted diseases (such as AIDS or HIV, gonorrhea, syphilis and others). Today it is almost impossible to distinguish people with AIDS or HIV. They are on treatment and overweight like any other healthy person.
5. An unwanted pregnancy (one becomes a mother or father before age).
6. Abortion attempts, which can have several consequences.

7. School dropout: suspend or stop your studies (for the girl) - This will cause a delay and even see a risk of failure for your future.
8. Losing the chances of forming a home in the future.
9. Having a child who will be educated outside of a conjugal home.
10. Shame and contempt for others (you lose the trust of friends).
11. Risk of unwanted marriage (forced to marry boy or girl because of pregnancy).
12. Loss of honor
13. A dysregulation of sexual desires that you can no longer control, etc....

Chapter XX

Your child should learn that any sexual act is not an expression of love and that all love will not result in a sexual act. Help the child understand that love is a feeling that can be expressed without an erotic impulse.

Love is a feeling that can fulfill or break lives; it all depends on what you do with it. Even those who sexually abuse others believe they are making love; and yet only a love lived in discipline and respect for others glorifies God and flourishes.

When your love for others always drives you to a sexual desire, this is already an anomaly.

You can explain this reality to the child with these three different Greek terms that describe love: *Agape, Phileo and Eros.*

Agape Love: is unconditional, deep and without desire. It is the love that God loves us with. It is a sacrificial love, which is ready to give everything without expecting anything in return. It is the love that God loved us in Jesus Christ. It is this love that unites us between brothers and sisters in the Lord; it does not engage our erotic feelings. It is an unnatural love, it is divine. We can only have it if the Lord Himself dwells in us by his Holy Spirit. It is difficult, and almost impossible, to live your own relationships, without scandal between girls and boys, between men and women, if you are not inhabited by Agape love.

It is the love that the Lord loved us, it is the love that unites us in Christ. This is why when people are in Christ, it is not difficult for them to live in continence until marriage. Agape love gives them pure feelings for each other.

Phileo love: Is a natural condition; human love between people who have certain things in common. Brothers, friends, for example people who grew up in the same neighborhood, having attended the same schools, colleagues from service, from duty, etc. It drives us to sharing and solidarity; while observing a certain reciprocity.

Eros love: Is sexual love which involves physical or erotic attraction. It is this love that leads to marriage. In the Christian conception of marriage, this love unites only two people of the opposite sex and not several; i.e. a man and a woman. Having Eros love towards anyone of the opposite sex is a serious anomaly; unfortunately, this is what happens with some people and this can only lead to sexual depravity, infidelity and disappointments. All Eros love outside of marriage is a sin. Eros love alone cannot sustain a home; the couple needs to add sacrificial agape love to their Eros love. Sincere forgiveness in a couple is only possible if both spouses are subject to unconditional love, the love which Christ loved us, Agape love.

Chapter XXI

Introduce children to the concept of friendship

The need for friendship is a natural and deep need for human life. There is a great need in human beings to lean on, to rely on someone or to share deeply with someone similar. It is the desire to commune with someone who is ready to give full attention, who is willing to go out of their way to find a solution when one is in difficulty and who even goes so far as to make sacrifices if necessary.

It is almost impossible in life to deal with everyone on an equal footing. In relationships we will always find people with whom we will develop a deeper friendship than with others. People who will give much more attention to who we are, to our opinions, and to situations than others.

The Bible, speaking of friendship, presents it as the best of relationships. God called many people to serve him

> **Friendship is the best of relationships**

in both the Old and New Testaments. To describe the very deep relationship there was between God and his servant Moses, the Bible says that God spoke to Moses as a man speaks to his friend. When Job was tested, the whole country did not come to spend time comforting him; it is more like friends. In his complaint he said: "He who suffers has the right to the compassion of his **friend**, even when he abandons the fear of the Almighty." By the way, we expect more from a friend than from everyone. Job shows that a friend's love is much more patient, tolerant than everyone's. Friendship is so important that the Bible shows us that even if a friend hurts us, we must prefer it over an enemy.

"A friend's wounds prove loyalty, but an enemy's kisses are deceiving." (Proverbs 27:6)

Chapter XXII

Even if you forget some lessons that you learned in these lines, here I present to you twelve truths which are like essential elements which you must remember.

1. As a parent, God has given you the privilege, the responsibility and the power to raise and train a child.

2.   Raising a child does not only consist in building his physical being, but also his inner person.

3.   Sexuality occupies a central place in human life; hence we cannot give a full education to the child, excluding his sexual education.

4.   Parents' harmony is an essential basis to support this education. The Bible says that a house divided against itself cannot stand.

5.   It is the responsibility of the parent (mother or father) to give their child a sex education, related to their Christian faith (Do not wait for the school or the street to do it for you).

6.   Giving your child a sex education would save them from sexual abuse and all kinds of false information going around.

7.   Each parent should make an effort to know the different topics to be covered in sex education so that they know what to say and when to say it to their child.

8.   The parent must break the silence & never be ashamed to start the discussion or the conversations with your child.

9.   Sex education should start in early childhood. God has already provided a natural space where the child is open for the parent to begin sex education with the child.

10.   Do not be trapped by taboos and do not perpetuate silence so that the future generation does not suffer from what we suffered ourselves.

11.   The sooner you start sex education, the easier it will be later.

12.   God is and will remain the foundation on which this education must be built. Be inspired by God and the Holy Scriptures.

One more thing

The parent must grow with the growth of his child and increase his knowledge in order to teach his child well. He must also improve the quality of the relationship that unites him with his child, to allow him to communicate better with him. Do not have an aggressive and chaotic relationship with the child. Do not be ashamed or hesitant to develop frank conversations to equip them.

The growth of the child is a school, and an opportunity for the parent to also grow in his responsibilities. Therefore, the parent must give his time to provide this education to his child. An absent parent, who is replaced by servants or third parties, without realizing it, will become a stranger to his own children and vice versa.

The path to healing

For children or adults who have experienced sexual abuse, the search for a cure remains an essential step. Why?

First: to help this victim regain self-confidence and pride in living. God is able to take away any feeling of contempt that has been attached to his life and restore it.

Second: so that they in turn are not tempted to abuse others. If the victim does not open up to seek help, he will be plagued by the abuses he has known, at the risk of becoming in turn a predator.

Third: so that they have the courage to forgive and report their abuser. To forgive your abuser is to free yourself from its grip, it is to erase it from your memory, it is no longer to give it the power to dominate over you through memories of

> Even if the WOUND seems painful and indelible, HEALING is possible

past abuses. To report the abuser is to defeat him, it is to end his activity, it is to expose his evil in broad daylight and prevent him from continuing to make new victims.

Fourth: so that the victim ceases to live in the past, to continually cry over the events of the past that they allow themselves to be taught and that they in turn become an educator.

Giving a child sex education, remains the single most secure way to pass on our values from one generation to the next. Each child who has been educated in this way will walk with their heads held high, will in turn become an educator and will remain grateful for the rest of their lives.

Restoration International Embassy

Restoration International Embassy is an apostolic and multicultural service of SRMI, headquartered in the United States of America. Our goal is to make various multisectoral, cross-cultural and international connections aimed at the salvation of souls, the awakening of believers, the restoration of nations by the proclamation and practice of redemption in Christ, by the formation and the ignition of ministers of the Gospel.

Connection is our specialty:
-Connect men with God, and with each other
-Connect the ministers of God with the harvest of the world
-Connect the needy with divine provision.

Our Mission is to raise, train and ignite Ambassadors for Christ for the restoration of the nations.

Our Action is: Reach - Equip - Connect
-Reach the unreached by personal witness, by missionary actions and the evangelization of the masses.
-Equip believers, by creating aid and training centers for leaders and missionaries.
-Connecting people with God and with each other, connecting ministers with the global harvest, and connecting the needy with divine provision. Serve as a bridge between peoples through various services and community actions.

One of RIE's activities is the organization of the *Global Emerging Missionaries Summit*

www.cross.tv/restoration_international_embassy
www.**RESTORATIONTOP.NET**

IshahPurpose International
Les Aides Semblables International

Initiated in 1995 by Pastor Astrid SONI, the ministry 'Les Aides Semblables International' (ASI), also known as **Ishah Purpose International**(IPI) is dedicated to helping women ministers and servants of God and equipping female leaders with various works.

Ishah Purpose International /ASI) is an interdenominational service to women on the front lines in their ministries: adults and youth serving the Lord, as well as the wives of God's ministers. This ministry is essentially active to:

- enhance the image of the servants of God and the women of the Servants of God,

- sharpen their potentials because of their significant role in the destiny of several churches and ministries.

-incite them to self-esteem, maturity and excellence in life.

Motivation and encouragement for individual fulfillment, mutual aid and excellence are the essential elements of our communion. (Proverbs 27:17).

ASI's mission to these ladies is to size them to the size and level of these ministries to which they are called to perform or assist.

Our watchword: "Equal to the task"

www.aidesemblables.com
Facebook.com/les aides semblables

WORKS PUBLISHED by

Grave la Vision

1.*Comme le fer aiguise le fer* (190 pages)

2.*Poèmes de Papa : Recueil des pensées et vers soufflés*(160 pages)

3.*Amazing Facts about the Holy Spirit*(300 pages)

4.*Le profil du leader*(162 pages)

5. *Guide pour Etudes Bibliques* Volume I (150 pages)

6.*La Sécheresse Spirituelle et la Rétrogradation*(Vol. I & II)

7. *Connaitre la volonté de Dieu et le but de votre vie*(170 pages)

8.*L'Enfer*(84 pages)

9.*Questions sur le Salut, la Sainteté et la Sécurité*(174 pages)

10.*Pleurs des Plaies*(148 pages)

11.*De tout cœur pour toute oreille*(150 pages)

12.*La Personne et l'œuvre de Jésus-Christ*(105 pages)

13.*Principes de la Restauration* (316 pages)

Works by Pastor **Astrid Mutha Soni**

Works by **Debbie Soni:**

1. *Memories: Lod'sPuzzle*(187 pages)
2. *The Ten Children of Celeste Pastry*(96pages)

Music:

-*J'ai Décidé*(CD audio avec 8 chants composés et écrits par Pasteur Astrid Soni& Soni Steps Music)

Publishers **Grave la Vision** are dedicated to helping authors publish their works: From conception to publication, including proofreading, editing, image capture, presentation and design of works (books, CDs , DVD, posters, leaflets).

www.gravelavision.com
Email : gl2020vision@gmail.com

Listen to our Radio online 24/7
www.restorationtop.net
Multilingual and transgenerational online radio

Parenting and Sex Education

Breaking the silence and ignorance
Challenging and removing the taboos
Preventing and healing the abuses

Sex education in the family is an effective way to protect children against sexual abuse and bad influences. The parents' silence is an open door to sexual abuse of children. Every child who haven't received this education is naïve and vulnerable. A sexually abused child risks carrying the conse-quences of this heinous act for the rest of his life. Hence, parents must save them at all costs.

Talking about sex education is not a cultural matter, it is rather a divine duty.

Astrid Mutha Soni

Minister of the Word, author, songwriter, marital counselor and men-tor of women and young ladies; passionate for human development, and specialist on life education.

A spouse of Dr Soni Mukwenze, the visionary and Bishop of *Restora-tion Church*, a holistic work they both initiated and lead as a couple. Pastor Astrid is also the vice-president of *Restoration International Embassy and SRMI*, and the founder and international president of *Aides Semblables International*, an organization devoted at the em-powerment of women and young girls.

International conference speaker frequently on the road, she is based in the USA with her husband and their four children.

Contact her through www.RESTORATIONTOP.NET

Grave la vision
A division of Soni Steps
Inspirational / Education

65793779R00102